A Voters' Rights Amendment

A Voters' Rights Amendment

• • •

Beyond *Citizens United*

John Kellett & Christine Kellett

ISBN-13: 9781530189212
ISBN-10: 1530189217

Acknowledgments

John Kellett wishes to thank his colleagues at Gettysburg College who read the manuscript and provided encouragement and helpful comments: Jean Holder, Bruce Boenau, and Ken Mott all read multiple drafts of the text and engaged in follow-up discussions that improved and helped shape the text. In addition, Carey Moore and Dave Crowner read early drafts and provided many helpful suggestions.

Table of Contents

Preface

In its 2010 decision *Citizens United v. Federal Election Commission* (FEC), the Supreme Court declared that corporations are persons, and as such are entitled to First Amendment rights. This decision essentially struck down campaign finance laws, thus assuring that big money's influence on the electoral process of the United States now goes virtually unchecked. In the years since that decision, a growing movement has been formed to amend the Constitution in order to overturn *Citizens United* and to remove the corrupting influence that the plutocracy now has over our electoral process. The proposed constitutional amendment—which declares that corporations are not persons, and that corporate political expenditures to buy political influence are not a form of constitutionally protected speech—is an essential first step in the return of democracy to the people. *Citizens United* was the result of a corrupted political environment: an overly evolved political environment that favors the rich. While *Citizens United* enhances the plutocracy's control of the electoral process, the decision is more a symptom of a structurally corrupt electoral process than a cause. We have to address the structural weaknesses of the electoral process before we can expect to restore the health of our democracy.

The current structure of the electoral process gives the plutocracy undue control over many factors, including

- *candidate selection*, by controlling who can effectively run for elected office, and who will likely succeed;
- the *political conversation*, by limiting the topics that are meaningfully discussed, as well as the depth of such discussions; and
- the *franchise*, by limiting the number of voters who have a meaningful vote in congressional races, in the presidential primary races, and in the general presidential election, and by making it difficult for any voters who are not likely to support the corporate agenda to meaningfully participate in the electoral process.

This book advocates the adoption of a "Voters' Rights Amendment" (henceforth "VRA," not to be confused with the Voting Rights Act of 1965, which is discussed later on in the book). This proposed amendment would go beyond the problems of unfettered campaign financing and the absurd notion of corporate "personhood" in order to address systemic problems in our electoral process and to loosen the hold that money now has over our democracy. The goal of the VRA is to fundamentally reform our electoral process. This comprehensive amendment would give candidates who are not in the Democratic or Republican parties a fair chance to participate in the electoral process; ensure that all voters and all candidates will be able to participate in a fair and meaningful electoral process; provide voters with the opportunity to register their concerns through their votes, both in the primaries and in the general elections; and diminish the influence of big money on our elections so that democracy may be returned to the people.

People often hesitate to promote constitutional amendments on the reasonable assumption that such amendments will be extremely difficult (if not impossible) to have adopted. The issue to consider is not whether such an amendment will be adopted, but rather if the amendment should be discussed. For example, while the Equal Rights Amendment was not adopted, the effort to get it adopted fundamentally changed many attitudes, laws, and court decisions on women's rights. Simply advocating the adoption of the VRA will expose the plutocracy's various mechanisms of control over the electoral process. Discussing the amendment is similar to the step that an alcoholic takes when admitting that he or she is an alcoholic. Identifying the mechanisms of control, clarifying the inappropriateness of these mechanisms, and exposing the corrupting nature of these mechanisms on our democracy are essential first steps in restoring the health of our electoral process.

Specific issues and candidates are discussed only when necessary to illustrate current problems with the electoral process. Focusing attention on the plutocracy—the very rich who have sought (and achieved) substantial influence over the electoral process and governmental decision-making processes—makes it possible to paint a clear picture of how the mechanisms of control work, the need for corrective measures to combat that control, and the basic form that the corrective constitutional amendments should take. Focusing on the ill health of the electoral process will unite people who agree about the need to reform the electoral process and who can agree on the necessity of adopting the required constitutional amendments, even if their concerns about specific issues and candidates may differ.

The need for fundamental electoral change becomes apparent when we examine the broad disillusionment with the electoral process, the lack of meaningful discussion of important issues, the list of candidates we have to choose from, and the poor functioning of the government. Having a clear picture of how the plutocracy controls the electoral process, and having a draft of the necessary amendments that would allow voters to take control of that process, can ignite the passion that will be required to bring about reform.

Taking away the mechanisms of control of the present electoral process from the plutocracy will result in a seismic shift of power from the plutocracy to the people. Those in power will fight this shift with all they have. The primary effort of the very rich and the corporate-interest protectors who currently benefit from the unhealthy electoral process will focus on doing what they currently do to candidates who are not supportive of the corporate agenda: they will make every effort to ensure that these or similar proposals for reform are not given a fair hearing. Using the potential of social media to create a movement, however, we can send the message to legislators: voting for the VRA is mandatory if you expect success in your next election.

Chapter 1 describes how the plutocracy has gained control over the electoral process, and how the existing process is inconsistent with the ideals of the Founding Fathers and with the Constitution; this is followed by a discussion of the ways in which the current electoral process is inconsistent with the majority of previous Supreme Court decisions. The dissenting opinions from the current court are poignant in those places where the majority opinion strays from prior precedents and focuses on protecting the interests of the plutocracy.

Chapter 2 provides several criteria for comparing different voting systems and explains why our system (and similar voting systems) allow the plutocracy to control and corrupt the electoral process. We discuss a simple proposed change to the voting system called "approval voting," which in a direct way would heal some of the existing problems, and would allow for several other essential corrective measures.

Chapter 3 goes into detail on the plan for changing our electoral process. It proposes a draft of the VRA, which has fourteen sections, each of which addresses constitutional changes that will be necessary to remove plutocratic mechanisms of control over the electoral process.

In chapter 4, we provide a rationale for each section of the amendment. These rationales are not intended to be definitive, but instead to stimulate further discussion. We also explain how the sections work together and complement one another so that the total effect of the sections will be greater than the sum of the individual parts. When the sections are considered together, we can better understand the plutocracy's controlling methods under our current system, and the need for fundamental change becomes clear.

Throughout history, and now especially in the Middle East, the struggle for money and power by the few has corrupted governments around the world. These efforts have resulted in widespread suffering, and have made real democracy extremely difficult to initiate or sustain. The democracy of the United States is at risk as a result of the struggle by the few for more and more power and money. We need nonviolent means that are consistent with our traditions and constitution in order to renew, protect, and sustain the promise of our fragile democracy.

I

The Evolution of the Electoral Process

Justice Stevens quoted Alexander Hamilton in his 1995 Supreme Court opinion of *US Term Limits, Inc. v. Thornton*:

> The true principle of a republic is, that the people should choose whom they please to govern them... This great source of free government, popular election, should be perfectly pure, and the most unbounded liberty allowed.

The framers of the Constitution were conflicted when they wrote and proposed the adoption of the document. A significant number of them were torn between what they believed and stated to be the characteristics of an ideal democracy and what they believed would protect, preserve, and enhance their financial interests and those of the plutocracy. In order to assure the ratification of the Constitution, it was necessary for them to move far from their stated ideals: to restrict the right to vote to a specified class of white males, to have some people considered to be the property of their owners, and to allow the value of votes to be distorted by the indirect election of senators thus assigning different weights to votes and by the adoption of the Electoral College.

As a result of popular pressure, our democracy has gradually moved toward that original ideal over the years. The pressure for a healthy democracy has resulted in elected officials passing amendments to the Constitution that specify that people are not property; that the right to vote is a citizen's right, whether male or female; that the right to vote is to be protected by law, and free of poll taxes; by the removal of the "three-fifths" rule (which counted slaves as three-fifths of a person when taking censuses to determine congressional representation); and that senators are to be directly elected by the voters. In addition to these constitutional amendments that have moved the United States toward a healthier democracy, we have passed laws to protect a person's right to vote. The Supreme Court has issued opinions that have articulated the ideals consistent with a healthy democracy and has decided cases that protect the right of citizens to have a meaningful vote.

During several periods in our history, the rich have gained control of the electoral process, and the three branches of government (legislative, executive, and judicial) have cooperated to protect the interests of the rich and to protect the interests of corporations at the expense of the people's interests. These periods have led to the passage of several amendments to the Constitution to make corrections to the electoral process. We are clearly in one of these periods where corporate interests have gained excessive control of the electoral process and the governmental decision-making process. If we want to move on from this period in our history, we must pressure our representatives to pass corrective amendments to the Constitution.

The Right to Vote and Corporate Interests

Our right to a meaningful vote has been severely undermined, which has subverted the people's interests to corporate interests and the plutocracy's interests: the very rich whose "religion" dictates that it is best for the country that corporate interests are to be protected and advanced at all costs, and that this principle should be consistently and persistently proclaimed. Those who protect corporate interests are generally not people who consciously *want* to undermine the right to vote or to subvert the people's interests, but their rise to positions of power (and their success in those positions) would be seriously jeopardized if they failed to protect corporate interests. As a result, the corporate interests and their interests become one and the same.

The control of the electoral process works to ensure that these protectors are the nominees of the two main political parties: the Republican and Democratic parties. The electoral process is similar to selective breeding and scientific feeding in agriculture. The plutocracy selectively nominates and profoundly influences all political discussions in the electoral process—the feeding of information to the voters—and, at considerable expense, they scientifically prepare and carefully control the feeding of much of the information that guides our representatives in the federal decision-making process.

Such control of the electoral process results in a restriction of the electoral conversation so that corporate interests will not be seriously jeopardized by identifying people's interests that might conflict with corporate interests. This suppressed election conversation results in elected officials who are not held accountable for actions of theirs that advance the corporate agenda at the expense of the people's interest. This lack of accountability for acts performed while in office provides positive feedback to elected officials to preserve, protect, and legitimize the restricted conversation and the corrupt electoral process.

The Right to Vote and the Constitution

The dominance of corporate influence in the electoral process has resulted in democracy nullification that is inconsistent with our amended Constitution, with the stated ideals of the framers of the Constitution, and with virtually all Supreme Court interpretations of the Constitution until very recent times. Below are a few excerpts from Supreme Court opinions that describe characteristics of the electoral process that *are* consistent with the Constitution and with the framers' ideals for the Constitution and our democracy. We also describe a few of the current inconsistencies in the electoral process by referring to various Supreme Court opinions.

The Warren court opined in *Reynolds v. Sims* (1963), with Chief Justice Warren writing the opinion of the court:

Undeniably the Constitution of the United States protects the right of all qualified citizens to vote... A consistent line of decisions by this Court in cases involving attempts to deny or restrict the right of suffrage has made this indelibly clear. It has been repeatedly recognized that all qualified voters have a constitutionally protected right to vote, and to have their votes counted.

In *Bush v. Gore* (2000), a five-to-four decision, the five protectors of corporate interests on the Supreme Court decided that the votes in Florida did not have to be counted to decide who would be president; rather, they decided that they could decide the outcome of the 2000 presidential race. These five justices declared George Bush to be the victor. Each of these five justices decided that it was his or her right to determine who would win the election; a switch of any one of the five justices' votes would have protected, in Warren's words, "the voters' constitutionally protected right to vote, and to have their votes counted." The five justices had good reason to question candidate Al Gore's credentials as a corporate-interest protector: he had demonstrated a deep concern for the environment by writing *Earth in the Balance* in 1992—a book that made the *New York Times* best-seller list.

Corporate Personhood

Corporate "DNA" goes back to the early colonial period, as a grant of privilege extended by the Crown to a group of investors: usually to finance a trade expedition and to limit the liability of investors to the amount of their investment (a privilege not held by ordinary citizens). The recognized purpose for the investors was (and remains) to generate capital and profits, limit risks, and limit liability. Corporate personhood evolved; it adapted to the financial opportunities that were made available by pressuring government to expand this special privilege by limiting taxes, regulations, and corporate responsibilities, and by severely curtailing liability and any political conversations that might adversely affect corporate interests. At times, the government even assumed the risk for corporate losses.

The corporate-interest protectors on the Supreme Court further assisted the evolution of corporate personhood in the *Citizens United v. FEC* decision in a way that is inconsistent with the intent of the framers and is inconsistent with previous Supreme Court interpretations. Since Theodore Roosevelt's presidency, numerous people have successfully pressured Congress to pass legislation to limit any corporate spending that is designed to influence the electoral process. These laws have been constitutionally tested in cases before the Supreme Court and have been found to be consistent with the Constitution. In 2010, however, corporate protectors succeeded in bringing about a major change in campaign financing. In a five-to-four decision, the Supreme Court declared in *Citizens United v. FEC* that Congress cannot pass laws that infringe on the "free speech rights of Corporations." In an editorial, the *New York Times* stated that "The Supreme Court has handed lobbyists a new weapon. A lobbyist can now tell any elected official: if you vote wrong, my company…will spend unlimited sums explicitly advertising against your re-election." The paper might have added that if elected officials or candidates even speak out meaningfully against corporations' interests, corporations (which are often publicly held but controlled by small executive groups) will spend unlimited sums of money to explicitly advertise against their reelections or elections. It is this threat that controls the speech of those who would otherwise speak out to protect the public interest.

Justice Stevens concluded his dissenting opinion in *Citizens United v. FEC* with the following:

> At bottom, the Court's opinion is thus a rejection of the common sense of the American people, who have recognized a need to prevent corporations from undermining self-government since the founding, and who have fought against the distinctive corrupting potential of corporate electioneering since the days of Theodore Roosevelt. It is a strange time to repudiate that common sense. While American democracy is imperfect, few outside the majority of this Court would have thought its flaws included a dearth of corporate money in politics.

In 1857, in *Dred Scott v. Sanford*, the Supreme Court held that Congress could not pass laws that would infringe on the property rights of slave owners. The court determined that slaves were property and that those property rights were protected by the Constitution. This decision gave rise to much of the agitation that led to the Civil War four years later. The Supreme Court's *Citizens United v. FEC* decision is the mirror image of the property rights of the *Dred Scott* case: *Dred Scott* made people property, while *Citizens United* made property people. The Supreme Court held in *Citizens United* that corporate property enjoys constitutionally protected personhood rights, and that Congress cannot pass laws that will infringe on the free speech rights of corporations. The court thus endowed a person's constitutional right to free speech upon corporate property. This right to speak (and to spend large amounts of corporate money) in order to influence the outcome of elections is exercised by corporate CEOs, and not by the workers or shareholders of the corporation. In some cases, the CEO is not a US citizen, while in other cases the CEO is a US citizen whose primary financial interests lie within foreign countries.

Another recent Supreme Court decision has further evolved and enhanced the corporate "person's" ability to compete in and enhance corporations' influence over the federal electoral process. In *McCutcheon v. FEC* (2014), a five-to-four decision, five Supreme Court justices expanded corporations' free speech and personhood rights by abolishing aggregate limits on direct financial contributions to candidates in federal elections. In his dissenting opinion, Justice Breyer stated:

> Where enough money calls the tune, the general public will not be heard. Insofar as corruption cuts the

link between political thought and political action, a free marketplace of political ideas loses its point.

In *Citizens United*, the same five Supreme Court justices stated in their opinion that "speech is an essential mechanism of democracy, for it is the means to hold officials accountable to the people." Who are these "people" they are referring to? In the opinion of the five Supreme Court justices, corporate donations represent the constitutionally protected free speech in federal election campaigns. To understand the effect of the *McCutcheon* decision, simply modify this quote by one word, to "*money* is an essential mechanism of democracy, for it is the means to hold officials accountable to corporate donors." Justice Breyer had more to say in his dissent:

> The result...is a decision that substitutes judges' understandings of how the political process works for the understanding of Congress; that fails to recognize the difference between influence resting upon public opinion and influence bought by money alone; that overturns key precedent; that creates huge loopholes in the law; and that undermines, perhaps devastates, what remains of campaign finance reform.

These five justices are politically astute. They fully recognize the difference between influence that rests upon public opinion and influence that is bought by money, but they chose to further enhance the plutocracy's ability to buy special access and influence. Again, to quote Justice Breyer (omitting internal citations for the sake of simplicity):

> The "appearance of corruption" can make matters worse. It can lead the public to believe that its efforts to communicate with its representatives or to help sway public opinion have little purpose. And a cynical public can lose interest in political participation altogether. "[T]he cynical assumption that large donors call the tune could jeopardize the willingness of voters to take part in democratic governance." Democracy, the Court has often said, cannot work unless "the people have faith in those who govern."

In 1818, Mary Shelley had Victor Frankenstein create an iconic monster out of different body parts; these five Supreme Court justices have created a real monster—with constitutionally protected rights—out of paper parts.

It is easier to discuss the corporate protection role played by the Supreme Court than it is to examine the role played by the other two branches of the federal government, since these branches work in the shadows. While Supreme Court justices have to justify their support in written opinions if those opinions are to be effective, the other two branches of government can often cover their corporate protection actions by issuing misleading descriptions of their activities. Congress and the executive branch of government have recently played particularly effective roles in advancing corporate interests, but they have put forth misleading cover stories. The corporate media has cooperated in this endeavor by focusing on distracting issues, promoting the corporate agenda, and repeating those political cover stories.

Third-Party Candidates and the Right to Vote

The lack of real opportunities for third-party candidates in the electoral process is another example that conflicts with the ideals stated by the framers of the Constitution, and with the stated ideals in various Supreme Court opinions. Justice Douglas stated in a concurring opinion in *Lubin v. Panish* (1974):

> But the right to vote would be empty if the State could arbitrarily deny the right to stand for election... "No right is more precious in a free country than that of having a voice in the election of those who make the laws under which, as good citizens, we must live. Other rights, even the most basic, are illusory if the right to vote is undermined."

When it does mention third-party candidates (which is not often), the mainstream media generally concentrates its attention on the candidate's possible "spoiler" effect, rather than on the issues that candidate raises. Third-party candidates often discuss issues that are antagonistic to the corporate agenda. Judging from mainstream news media coverage, any discussion of these issues has no place in our electoral process, even when the polls show that a majority of the public is interested in these issues. Real discussions of important national issues that would conflict with the corporate agenda are absent from the federal electoral process, and thus from the formulation of governmental policy.

The first line of defense for protecting corporate rights is to make it expensive and legally difficult to gain ballot access. The second line of defense is to create ambiguous rules for participation in presidential debates, thus leaving considerable room for political party bosses to make the "right" decisions. As Justice Souter opined in *Norman v. Reed* (1992):

> For more than two decades, this Court has recognized the constitutional right of citizens to create and develop new political parties. The right derives from the First and Fourteenth Amendments, and advances the constitutional interest of likeminded voters to gather in pursuit of common political ends, thus enlarging the opportunities of all voters to express their own political preferences.

Citizens face extreme difficulties in creating and developing new political parties. Protectors of the corporate interests can (and do) block any chances to enlarge voters' opportunities to express their political preferences. Voters' ability to show their political preferences with their votes is severely constrained by the corporate-interest protectors' control of the electoral process, and their ability to limit the information that voters base their votes upon.

The political party bosses' control of the regulations that govern the electoral process devalues most of the votes, both in the primaries and in the general election. The states—which are influenced by the political party bosses of both the Republican and Democratic parties—have passed a variety of heterogeneous ballot access laws, which makes it extremely difficult for third-party candidates to gain ballot access. As we mentioned earlier, this is inconsistent with the ideals stated by the framers of the Constitution and with the stated ideals of many Supreme Court opinions. As Justice Stevens wrote in delivering the opinion of the court in *US Term Limits, Inc. v. Thornton* (1995):

> Our opinion made clear that this broad principle incorporated at least two fundamental ideas. First, we emphasized the egalitarian concept that the opportunity to be elected was open to all...Second, we recognized the critical postulate that sovereignty is vested in the people, and that sovereignty confers on the people the right to choose freely their representatives to the National Government.

The opportunity to be elected is not open to all. If you do not feel comfortable being a Democrat or Republican, your chance of running a successful campaign for president is nil. Even the opportunity to run a campaign where your voice will be heard on the issues is nil. This corruption of the electoral process by restricting non-Republican and non-Democratic candidates from a fair chance to participate in

John Kellett & Christine Kellett

the electoral process has also been called into question by
various Supreme Court opinions. In *Williams v Rhodes* (1968),
for example, Justice Black expressed the opinion of the court
thus:

> The right to form a party for the advancement of
> political goals means little if a party can be kept off
> the election ballot, and thus denied an equal opportu-
> nity to win votes. So also, the right to vote is heavily
> burdened if that vote may be cast only for one of two
> parties when other parties are clamoring for a place
> on the ballot.

In addition, the two main parties put considerable effort
into denying third-party candidates the opportunity to participate in debates. The presidential debates during general
presidential elections are produced, directed, and staged by
the Democratic and Republican political party bosses. The
debates are managed to minimize the chances that conversations will take place that might jeopardize corporate interests. Finally, if a third-party candidate does succeed in being
allowed to participate in the presidential debates—usually
with the help of one of the main parties, but only because
its bosses feel the spoiler effect will help its prospects—then
the candidate is still given minimal opportunities to discuss
issues that might adversely affect corporate interests and the
mainstream media gives minimal coverage to discussions of
the issues.

Suppressing the Right to a Meaningful Vote

Most voters do not have a meaningful vote in choosing the nominees for president. If you are a Democrat or a Republican who is running for office, but you are not extremely rich or do not have the support of the political party bosses or the big money interests, you have virtually no chance of being considered a top-tier candidate in the critical early primaries.

The result is that during primary races, the field of candidates is limited to one or two protectors of the corporate interests before most people even have the chance to vote. The viable top-tier candidates are careful not to discuss in any meaningful way any of the people's issues that might conflict with corporate interests. During general elections, the field is reduced to two viable corporate-protection candidates from the two main political parties; there is still little to no meaningful discussion of the important opportunities and challenges that face the nation. The mainstream media continues to focus on the race, rarely if ever bringing up any issues that the mainstream candidates have chosen to ignore.

Furthermore, the right of suffrage has been denied to a significant percentage of the voters by the disproportionate assignment of delegates during primary races, and the disproportionate assignment of electoral votes during general presidential elections. The use of a "winner takes all" system for Electoral College votes (which is the situation in most states) substantially reduces the number of voters who have a say in the outcome of elections; the system also makes it virtually impossible for third-party candidates to win electoral votes.

This reduction of meaningful votes leads to the concentration of political spending in a few key states; this concentration of money enhances the value of money in determining the outcome of the race, and it makes candidates more reliant on support from big money for their success. After the Republican and Democratic nominations in the 2012 presidential campaign, more campaign advertising dollars were spent in Nevada, New Hampshire, and Iowa (with a total population of less than five million) than were spent in California, Texas, and New York (with a total population of more than seventy million). The outcome in the big states was almost assured—even before the candidates were nominated—as a result of winner-take-all electoral votes and because of the unevenness of the voter alignment within the Republican and Democratic parties in each of the large population states. In such cases, voters from big states who are members of the minority party—for instance, Democrats in Texas or Republicans in New York—will have reason to believe that their participation in presidential elections will be meaningless.

The corrupting effect of the electoral process by the "dilution of the weight of a citizen's vote" (to quote Chief Justice Warren) is inconsistent with the Constitution, as stated in the following excerpt from the landmark case that assured one vote per person. Warren, expressing the opinion of the court for *Reynolds v. Sims* (1964), wrote that:

[T]he right of suffrage can be denied by a debasement or dilution of the weight of a citizen's vote just as effectively as by wholly prohibiting the free exercise of the franchise.

The political party bosses are the major players in making the rules for the assignment of delegates in the primaries, and for the assignment of electoral votes in general elections. This is an example of the indirect denial of a voter's right to meaningfully participate in presidential elections, and is inconsistent with our constitutional rights. Justice Souter addressed this issue in writing the opinion for the Supreme Court in *US Term Limits, Inc. v. Thornton* (1995): "As we have often noted, 'constitutional rights would be of little value if they could be…indirectly denied.'"

Distracting Attention and Energizing the Base of Support

Recent Supreme Court decisions have affected the political conversation and political support by focusing on certain constituencies; this energizes the base of support for candidates who are corporate-interest protectors on the basis of certain cultural issues (some of which are discussed below). Such a focus makes it possible to avoid explicit discussion of those corporate interests that conflict with the people's interests.

The Pulitzer Prize–winning journalist Linda Greenhouse, who reported on the Supreme Court for the *New York Times* from 1978 to 2008 and now teaches at Yale Law School, wrote about the court in the op-ed pages of the *New York Times* in May 2014:

The problem is...that it's too often simply wrong: wrong in the battles it picks, wrong in setting an agenda...wrong in refusing to give the political system breathing room to make fundamental choices of self-governance...The Supreme Court itself has become an engine of polarization, keeping old culture-war battles alive and forcing to the surface old conflicts that people were managing to live with.

Some of these polarizing issues that the Supreme Court has recently chosen to address include the gun issue (*District of Columbia v. Heller* and *McDonald v. Chicago*); race (*Shelby Country v. Holder*); religion (*Town of Greece v. Galloway* and *Burwell v. Hobby Lobby Stores, Inc.*); and women's rights issues (*Walmart v. Dukes, McCullen v. Coakley, and Gonzales v. Carhart*). Much of the campaign spending by the plutocracy furthers this polarization by focusing on issues that do not seriously affect corporate interests. These polarizing political discussions often make it possible for the Democratic and Republican candidates to avoid discussing the compromises that need to be made between the corporate interests and the people's interests. The political polarization and the paucity of discussions about the need for compromise result in the federal government's failure to address many of the challenges that face the nation.

The compromises that need to be made before we can hope to balance corporate interests and the people's interests need to be discussed and implemented at the federal level. Because states compete for corporate spending, it is difficult to pass legislation that would call for corporate protection of the people's interests at the state level.

Citizen Influence vs. Corporate Influence

In July 2015, Lawrence Lessig, professor of law at Harvard University, wrote in the *New York Times*:

> For the first time in modern history, the leading issue concerning voters in the upcoming [2016] presidential election, according to a *Wall Street Journal/NBC News* poll, is that "wealthy individuals and corporations will have too much influence over who wins."

When the Constitution was written in 1787, the main tension that the framers had to grapple with was the right way to balance the power of the states versus the power of the federal government; today, the main tension in the functioning of government stems from the battle between the people's say in the governing process versus corporate influence in determining how elections are run, and in finding a balance between corporate interests and the people's interests.

We have become accustomed to our traditional electoral process: so much so that we believe that this is the way it should be done and has to be done. But it does not have to be done this way, nor should it be done this way: a way that allows the plutocracy to control and further corrupt the electoral process.

II
Voting Systems

The voting system used most often in the United States is called *plurality voting*. A comparison of different voting systems shows that the plutocracy exploits weaknesses in this voting system to protect and advance its interests and to enhance its control of the election process. In this chapter, we describe and compare runoff voting, instant runoff voting, plurality voting, and approval voting. In the past, these voting systems have been considered primarily in terms of the fairness of the vote count; here we also consider the effect of the voting system on the process of vetting candidates for office. The selection of a voting system profoundly affects the fairness, effectiveness, and public exposure of candidate vetting, which are the primary determinants of the health of our democracy. Our main focus is on approval voting, a system whose adoption would make it possible for the people to regain control of the election process and to wrest control from the hands of the plutocracy. We begin with a discussion of other voting systems.

Runoff Elections

Runoff elections may (and often do) involve two rounds of voting. In the first round, if no candidate wins a majority of the votes, then the two leading candidates run against each other in the second round. A few states use this type of election in their gubernatorial races and in local elections; many other countries also use the system in presidential elections. The system often results in the initial runoff candidates winning the election with less than 30 percent support, and subsequently suffering strong disapproval ratings. This is the result of the "split vote" problem in the first round of the election—i.e., several candidates who have similar appeal split the vote, and fringe candidates emerge as the winners as a result. While such runoff elections give the illusion of majority support, such "support" is simply the result of the process being reduced to two candidates. Consider the following recent examples.

The 2012 Egyptian presidential election used a runoff electoral process. Mohamed Morsi, the Muslim Brotherhood candidate, and Ahmed Shafik, the prime minister from the overthrown Hosni Mubarak administration, were the two candidates in the runoff election. Thirteen candidates participated in the first round, and, as a result of the split-vote problem, the top two candidates both had less than 25 percent support during the first round. In numerous polls leading up to the election, Morsi, the winner in the runoff, consistently had less than 20 percent support, and often less than 10 percent; he received 51 percent of the votes in the runoff election, however. This support is misleading, as it only measures his support in comparison to Shafik: neither candidate had broad support, and each had strong disapproval ratings. Following these ostensibly fair elections—the first in many decades in Egypt—Morsi was unable to govern due to his lack of broad support. He was forced out of office by a public uprising that threatened, and possibly destroyed, the democratic process in Egypt.

In the 2002 French election, so many left-wing and moderate candidates ran in the first round of voting that two right-wing candidates managed to advance to the second round. In the first round, Jacques Chirac received 20 percent, and Jean-Marie Le Pen came in second, with 16.9 percent support. Lionel Jospin, a socialist, had 16.1 percent support in the first round as a result of the split-vote problem on the left. In the runoff election, Chirac received 82 percent of the vote to Le Pen's 18 percent. Political analysts believed that a runoff between Chirac and Jospin would have been a real contest to determine public support; Le Pen was a fringe candidate who never had more than 18 percent support in the polls.

Our plurality voting process in early presidential primaries in small states results in the rapid narrowing of the field of candidates as a result of split votes similar to the problems in runoff elections. Candidates who have more than 20 percent (but often less than 30 percent) support become the focus of attention: the so-called top-tier candidates. The plutocracy effectively capitalizes on this situation by concentrating campaign spending in the early primaries in order to advance candidates who can be relied upon to protect its interests.

Instant Runoff Voting

Using an instant runoff voting system, voters rank the candidates as their first, second, and third choices. If one candidate has a majority of first-choice votes when the votes are counted, then that candidate wins. If no candidate has gained a majority of votes, then the candidate with the fewest number of first-choice votes is dropped, and his/her votes are distributed (in terms of the voters' second choices), and these votes then get counted as first-choice votes. This process continues until one of the candidates has a majority of the votes.

The following example illustrates how this voting method works. For illustration purposes we assume that there are one hundred voters. This is a simplification of the voting process, but it illustrates the problems that may arise. The table below describes the ballots.

Table 5: Ballot description

Choice	44 ballots	32 ballots	13 ballots	6 ballots	5 ballots
First	Smith	Lloyd	Jones	Brown	Brown
Second	Brown	Smith	Brown	Jones	Smith
Third	Jones	Brown	LLoyd	Loyd	Jones

Note that all thirty-two voters who voted for Lloyd as their first choice also voted for Smith as their second choice and Brown as their third choice. Brown's first-choice voters are separated into two columns, since their second and third choices differ; six of the voters who voted for Brown as their first choice voted for Jones as their second choice and Lloyd as their third choice, and five of the voters who voted for Brown as their first choice voted for Smith as their second choice and Jones as their third choice. All forty-four voters who voted for Smith as their first choice also voted for Brown as their second choice and Jones as their third choice.

Applying instant runoff voting, after counting all ballots, no candidate has a majority. Thus, as illustrated below in Table 6, the candidate with the fewest first-choice votes (Brown, with eleven) is dropped. Jones picks up six, so his count is now nineteen. Smith picks up five, so now his count is forty-nine.

Table 6: Vote count (Brown dropped)

Choice	49 ballots	32 ballots	19 ballots
First	Smith	Lloyd	Jones
Second	Jones	Smith	Lloyd
Third	[none]	[none]	[none]

Again, since no candidate has a majority, the lowest of the surviving candidates is dropped: Jones is dropped, and his nineteen votes go to Lloyd, since Brown is no longer a candidate. The table below shows that Lloyd now has fifty-one votes, a majority, and he is declared the winner.

Table 7: Final vote count (Brown dropped)

Choice	51 ballots	49 ballots
First	Lloyd	Smith
Second	Smith	Jones
Third	[none]	[none]

The above example illustrates the shortcomings of the instant runoff voting method of voting. First, the voters cannot know the significance of their ranking when they cast their votes; this can only be known when the votes are counted. Second, the winner does not necessarily have the highest level of first-choice support, or even the highest level broad-based support. Third, it is difficult to rank candidates: for example, whom do you rate first, the candidate you most prefer, or the one whom you believe has the best chance of defeating your "nightmare" candidate? Fourth, a candidate's standing in the political polls is a significant factor in a candidate's ability to raise money and to gain the attention of both the voters and the media—when using instant runoff voting, polls that measure voter support during the campaign will be ambiguous about voter support, since it will be impossible to interpret the relative value of voter support when voters are asked to rank the candidates.

The illustration above shows that Smith had significantly more first-choice votes and significantly more second-place votes than Lloyd; that Smith's total of first- and second-choice votes was greater than Lloyd's total of first-, second, and third-choice votes; and that Jones and Brown also had greater total vote counts than the winner, Lloyd.

Approval Voting

In the approval voting method, voters have the option to vote for as many candidates as they like, and each vote is counted as a single vote. Approval voting allows voters to express their preferences and concerns more clearly, and the resulting vote count is a better measure of voter preferences. Approval voting encourages a broader, less negative, and more in-depth discussion of the issues, and it eliminates the possibility of candidates becoming spoilers or having the "spoiler" label attached to their candidacies. Approval voting eliminates the problem in which candidates who have similar appeal split their voter support, thus distorting the measure of their support. The advantages of approval voting will be discussed in detail in chapter 4.

If we assume that the voters in the above Instant Runoff example were voting using the approval voting method, and that they would approve of their first- and second-choice candidates, then the result of the voting would be as illustrated in the table below:

Table 8: Totals using approval voting: first and second choices approved

	Lloyd	Jones	Brown	Smith
Approval voting totals	32	19	68	81

Note that the winner of the instant runoff voting method—Lloyd—comes in a distant third when using approval voting.

If we assume that the voters in the above example were voting using approval voting and that they would approve of their first-, second-, and third-choice candidates, then the result of the voting would be as indicated in Table 9 below:

Table 9: Totals using approval voting: first, second, and third choices approved

	Lloyd	Jones	Brown	Smith
Approval voting totals	51	68	100	81

Note that Lloyd, who was the winner when using the instant runoff voting method, comes in a distant last, and Brown is the new winner.

Plurality Voting

Plurality voting, currently the most commonly used voting method, is similar to instant runoff voting, but it has more severe shortcomings than that method. Voting in the primaries is very similar to instant runoff voting, in that the candidates who receive the lowest percentage of the votes in the early primaries are out (or effectively out) of the race, since voters do not want to waste their votes on candidates who have little chance of winning. This is true even if a voter likes a candidate's stance on the issues, and would like to show support for that candidate. In the later primaries, the lowest-performing candidate's support is divided among the other candidates, which is very similar to what happens in the instant runoff voting method. This process gets repeated in the early primaries, thus making the early primaries crucial (and effectively fatal) for most of the candidates. The illustration above shows that this process often chooses candidates who lack broad support.

The plurality voting system has other problems that instant runoff voting lacks. First, plurality voting in the presidential primaries results in a rapid collapsing of the field to only a few candidates, but it only involves voters from a few small states. Those voters are not able to indicate alternative choices—they have to vote for one candidate, based on very limited information. These voters also know that if they do not vote for a candidate who is leading in the polls— one whom the corporate media has identified as a top-tier candidate—then their votes are not likely to play a role in the election process, or in building support for particular issues. This artificial limiting of voting options drastically limits voters' ability to express their support for alternative candidates and to support those candidates' issues. This results not only in the collapsing of the field of candidates, but in drastically limited discussions of the issues.

Most of the candidates in the early 2016 Republican primaries strove to gain double-digit support in order to demonstrate that they were legitimate contenders; even gaining more than 2 percent support would demonstrate that they could be counted among the top tier of the Republican debaters. Candidates appealed directly to a minority of voters, making more radical commitments to particular issues than their rivals: a taller border fence, a more restrictive immigration policy, a bigger tax cut, a more aggressive military commitment, etc. The candidates successfully used these tactics to gain sufficient support to be considered "real" contenders (with more than 10 percent support), or at least to gain more than 5 percent support.

Before and during the early primaries, plurality voting focuses answers to poll questions on a voter's support for a single candidate, which distorts the relative level of voter support for other, perhaps second choice, candidates. These distortions in the polls influences the media coverage, fund-raising efforts, and discussions of issues of the candidates. The distortion in measuring relative support can also force the early termination of several candidates. For example, Wisconsin Governor Scott Walker dropped out of the primary race in September 2015; he indicated that the distortion in political polls was hurting both the selection process and the Republican Party. Walker suspended his campaign, explaining that "I believe that I am being called to lead by helping to clear the field in this race so that a positive, conservative message can rise to the top of the field."

Voters before and during the early primaries can often identify the candidates they will *not* be willing to support, but it is often extremely difficult to determine at this point in the vetting process which candidate might be the best choice to be president. The use of approval voting would focus poll questioning on those candidates whom the voters would like to remain in the race, thus indicating clearly those they would *not* want to support. Such a situation would result in a legitimate narrowing of the field of candidates.

The resulting misleading messages of the voting can and often does result in the winning candidate having low support for his or her governing policies: policies that were not well clarified in the election process. This process also limits the voters' opportunities to contribute to the establishment of national priorities, and it limits the accountability of the elected officials to the voters.

The political polls that lead up to the primaries are crucial for candidates; they significantly influence media coverage, as well as a candidate's ability to raise money. Because the polls are based on plurality voting, the polls can lead to significant problems. They often send misleading messages and result in poor corporate media coverage of certain campaigns.

The political polls from July 16, 2015, illustrate some of the problems that these polls may present. The polls indicated the following percentage support for the Democratic Party candidates: Clinton (59), Sanders (14), Biden (8), O'Malley (1), and Chafee (0); and for the leading Republican Party candidates they were Trump (17), Bush (14), Walker (8), Huckabee (7), Rubio (6), Carson (6), and Paul (6). Note that

Trump was the leader among the Republican field, and thus would have won the Republican primary had it been held that day. Another poll, however, asked how each of the leading Republican candidates would do in a presidential contest against Hillary Clinton. The results were the following:

- Clinton vs. Bush: 46 percent vs. 42 percent
- Clinton vs. Trump: 54 percent vs. **34** percent
- Clinton vs. Walker: 48 percent vs. 37 percent
- Clinton vs. Rubio: 46 percent vs. 40 percent
- Clinton vs. Paul: 48 percent vs. 38 percent
- Clinton vs. Huckabee: 49 percent vs. 42 percent
- Clinton vs. Carson: 49 percent vs. 36 percent

Note that Donald Trump, who was highest in the first poll question, was lowest in the two-person race with Hillary Clinton; this is a strong indication that his support was not broad-based. It is likely that Trump would be near the bottom of the list if one were to use approval voting and ask the question: "Who would you be willing to support among the listed candidates?"

Trump's standing in the polls took up much of the corporate media's attention in its 2016 political campaign coverage. The coverage focused on a few of his cultural statements and a few non-substantive personal statements about other candidates and media personnel, particularly *Fox News's* Megan Kelly.

The narrow range of support for the other Republican candidates (34 –42 percent) in the two-person contest with

Clinton is indicative of the public's lack of clarity on the candidates' stances on various issues. The splitting of support allows for a winning strategy based on name recognition, negative comments and advertising, and anything else that money can buy. Consider a different scenario where approval voting is used instead and the voters are asked, "Who would you be willing to support?" The voters' answers would result in each of them having an honest measure of their support (or their ability to gain support).

Summary

Our present voting system is like "No Child Left Behind," in that the scoring corrupts the process: the winning strategies are inconsistent with the purpose of the process. No Child Left Behind results in teachers teaching to the tests; the test grades of the class become the measure of success, the goal of the school, and the goal of teaching. Fostering the intellectual curiosity of all students, increasing their love of learning and their confidence in their ability to learn, and cultivating their ability and interest in searching for a better understanding of the world—these are no longer the goals of most schools.

The desirable attributes of a healthy electoral process get aggressively pushed aside with our grading system, plurality voting, and the existing rules governing the electoral process. Plurality voting focuses the voter's attention on one or two candidates from the main political parties. Most often, the political party candidates that emerge from the primaries are grateful to their corporate-interest protectors for their huge financial support—the support that was essential to achieving their top-tier candidate status. Continued financial support from the plutocracy in the general presidential election is important to a candidate's success.

The attention that is focused on only a few candidates, coupled with the states' disproportionate assignment of delegates, results in an early narrowing of the field of candidates. Delegate count is used at the nominating conventions to decide the political parties' nominees. In a healthy electoral process, delegates should be assigned to candidates in proportion to a fair measure of their voter support; this does not happen. Approval voting would allow for assigning delegates to each candidate in each state's primary in proportion to the candidate's *true voter support*. Voters would be able to vote on their real concerns without having to worry about "wasting" their vote.

Runoff elections, instant runoff elections, and plurality elections all focus attention on two candidates. The assignment of delegates via the running score card registers only the top-tier candidates on the score card. The unfair score card, the narrowing of the field of candidates, and the drastic narrowing of the political conversation before most voters even have the chance to vote are symptomatic of the unhealthy electoral process in the United States.

Similarly, in the general presidential elections, approval voting would allow for the honest measure of voter support for each candidate and a fair assignment of state electoral votes. Approval voting in the general election would allow more than two candidates to compete without the split-vote problem distorting the outcome of the election. Fair measuring of each candidate's support, fair assignment of delegates in the primaries, and fair assignment of electoral votes in the general elections would be major steps in freeing the electoral process from the corrupting control of the plutocracy. We propose a constitutional amendment called the Voters' Rights Amendment in the next chapter. Adopting approval voting is a first, essential step in denying the corporate-interest protectors the opportunities they now have to nullify the practice of democracy. Democracy and capitalism can both thrive side by side if the money interests are not allowed to control the electoral process.

We can restore the health of our democracy by insisting that our elected officials vote for the Voters' Rights Amendment.

III

A Voters' Rights Amendment

The following is a first draft of the Voters' Rights Amendment. The proposed VRA is divided into fourteen sections. A discussion of each section follows in the next chapter.

Section 1: Approval Voting

The President and members of Congress will henceforth be nominated and elected by approval voting. A voter may cast one vote for each candidate he or she approves of for the office that is being contested, and the votes will be counted in the usual way.

Section 2: Ballot Access

Congress shall establish ballot access laws. The requirements for ballot access for Congress and for the presidency will be uniform across all states.

Section 3: Presidential Debates

An independent Presidential Debate Board (henceforth "PDB"), appointed by the President and approved of by the Senate, will plan the presidential debates and will decide the number of debates, as well as their format and location and who does the questioning. If the PDB manages a political party's primary debates and the winning candidate achieves a specified level of voter support as set by Congress, the winning candidate will be assured ballot access in all states and the right to participate in the presidential debates. The aforementioned Presidential Debate Board will be subject to a recall vote at the time of the presidential election; if recalled, a new board will be appointed in its place.

Section 4: Independent Parties and Independent Voters' Primaries

The PDB will manage an independent voters' primary debate process leading up to the primary elections. Every state shall hold an Independent Voters' Primary for president; every political party that has achieved a specified level of support (to be set by Congress) and that has abided by the rules of the PDB shall be entitled to place a candidate or candidates on the independent voters' primary ballot.

The winner of the independent voters' primary election, and any other candidate who receives a specified level of support (to be set by Congress) in the primaries, shall be entitled to appear on all state ballots and to participate in the presidential debates.

Section 5: Media Oversight

(5a) In any presidential election year, public media will spend a significant amount of time interviewing presidential candidates and covering pertinent national issues. A Public Media Board (henceforth "PMB") appointed by the President and approved of by the Senate will select independent groups to lead discussions on public media and on government-purchased time on other media.

(5b) In the general presidential election campaigns, the PMB will partially fund private media so that candidates who are on all of the state ballots will have considerable opportunities to discuss national issues. The PMB will be adequately funded by the federal government. The PMB will be subject to a recall vote at the time of the presidential election; if recalled, a new board will be appointed.

Section 6: Recounts

In presidential elections, a presidential candidate may challenge the counting in any five congressional districts and acquire a supervised recount. If the count is substantially inaccurate, the count will not be considered to be one of the challenges.

Section 7: Voting Records

Control of vote counting will be at the voting district level, and paper records will be kept for at least one year following elections.

Section 8: The Electoral College

In presidential elections using approval voting, each candidate will be assigned electoral votes from each state in proportion to his/her voter support, rounded off to one decimal point. A candidate's voter support will be determined by dividing the number of votes each candidate receives by the total number of voters.

Section 9: Delegate Assignment

Following a presidential primary in which a political party uses approval voting, each candidate in the race will be assigned delegates to his/her party's national convention in proportion to his/her voter support.

Section 10: The Redistricting of Congressional Districts

The President, with the approval of the Senate, shall appoint a Redistricting Commission with staggered, fifteen-year terms for commission members. The commission will determine the broad principles (in consonance with the US Constitution) that will guide the redistricting of congressional districts after each new census, and will then supervise the process of redistricting so that the process remains consistent with the principles that have been set forth.

Section 11: Independent and Diverse Media

(11a) The Federal Communications Commission (FCC) and the aforementioned proposed Public Media Board will cooperate to direct the divestiture of mainstream media corporations from other corporations.

(11b) The FCC and the PMB will cooperate to ensure diversity of ownership of mainstream news media corporations.

Section 12: Protecting the Franchise

(12a) All states will facilitate the right to vote by ensuring minimal disruption in the verification of voter identity.

(12b) All states are required to provide convenient early voting in federal elections.

(12c) Felons who have completed their sentences will be allowed to vote.

Section 13: The Confirmation of Supreme Court Justices

(13a) A person nominated by the president to be a justice of the Supreme Court shall answer truthfully and fully all senators' questions about issues that may come before the Supreme Court. All information pertinent to the confirmation will be made available to the Senate. The minimum age of a candidate shall be sixty.

(13b) The Public Media Board will select several independent groups to lead discussions on public media (and on government-purchased time on other media) about the confirmation hearing and the arguments for and against confirmation. The PMB will have access to all information that is made available to the Senate.

Section 14: Repealing *Citizens United*

Congress has been asked to vote on this amendment as stated below, introduced by Representative McGovern of Massachusetts in 2015. The purpose was and is to repeal the Citizens United v. FCC *decision. Section 14 could be a separate constitutional amendment.*

14(a). We the people, who ordain and establish this Constitution, intend the rights protected by this Constitution to be the rights of natural persons.

14(b). The words *people, person,* or *citizen* as used in this Constitution do not include corporations, limited liability companies, or any other corporate entities established by the laws of any state, the federal government of the United States, or any foreign state. Such corporate entities are subject to such regulation as the people (through their elected state and federal representatives) deem reasonable and that are otherwise consistent with the powers of Congress and the states under this Constitution.

14(c). Nothing contained herein shall be construed to limit the people's rights of freedom of speech, freedom of the press, free exercise of religion, freedom of association, or any other such rights of the people, as these rights are inalienable. Congress shall have the power to make all laws necessary and appropriate to carry into effect all the foregoing sections of this Voters' Rights Amendment.

IV

Discussion of the Voters' Rights Amendment

The following chapter discusses the particulars of each section of the VRA in turn.

Section 1: Approval Voting

The president and members of Congress will henceforth be nominated and elected by approval voting. A voter may cast one vote for each candidate he or she approves of for the office that is being contested, and the votes will be counted in the usual way.

Reasons for Section 1
Approval voting eliminates the split-vote problem and assures that every candidate's support will be fairly recorded and not adversely impacted by other candidates in the race who have similar appeal. Approval voting assures several other essential sections to this amendment: a uniform ballot access section, a section that provides for an independent voters' primary for non-major-party candidates, and sections that require

the fair assignment of delegates in the primaries and the fair assignment of electoral votes in general elections.

Approval voting assures a fair polling of a candidate's support during the campaign, since the pertinent question to be asked when polling will be, "Which of the candidates do you approve of and could you support?" Polls that show the level of support during campaigns significantly affect the outcome of races; candidates who do not have a high level of support will have difficulty raising money for their campaigns, obtaining media coverage, and convincing voters to consider their messages. Removing these distortions in the level of support for candidates, especially early in their campaigns, (which results from voters having to consider only *one candidate* whom they will likely vote for) gives a better picture of the true level of support for each candidate.

In the early primaries, voters often lack sufficient information to answer the simple question, "Who will make the best president?" This is similar to the question, "Who will make the best spouse?" It is not a question that can be reliably answered with the level of information voters have. Most voters, however, can confidently state which of the candidates they would *not* want to be president. Approval voting would allow voters to show support for a candidate's position— even when they know that the candidate is likely to lose the election—without "wasting" their votes. This support could be crucial in influencing policies after the election, and may also be helpful in building coalitions to support various positions. Voters might want to support a candidate, even if they know the candidate will likely lose (and possibly not really wanting the candidate to win), because they feel that their voice on crucial issues should be heard. For example, Ron Paul spoke out in the 2012 Republican primary by taking positions on many issues that were not consistent with the corporate agenda. Some voters might have wanted to show support for him in order to keep his voice in the debates even if they did not expect or want him to win.

Approval voting would significantly improve the conversations leading up to elections. Such conversations educate the nation and help the voters determine how and by whom the country should be governed. Since approval voting makes it possible for voters to better express their concerns and preferences, the result is a fair showing of support for each candidate and their positions without the distortion of a split vote. As a result, such elections allow citizens to more directly and more effectively affect government policies.

The corporate agenda supporters have shaped the current primary process and the general elections so that the field of candidates is narrowed as quickly as possible. The goal is to eliminate those political party candidates who cannot be relied upon not to bring up topics that would recommend governmental actions that might adversely affect corporate interests. Approval voting is an essential part of the reform that will be required if we are to wrest control of the electoral process from the corporate-interest protectors. Several of the other proposed sections of the amendment require the adoption of approval voting in order to be effective.

Section 2: Ballot Access

Congress shall establish ballot access laws. The requirements for ballot access for Congress and for the presidency will be uniform across all states.

Reasons for Section 2

The federal courts have allowed states to severely limit ballot access for congressional and presidential candidates. The bases for the courts' rulings have been the split-vote problem. Such a problem does not exist with approval voting. The support of each candidate is registered fairly, even if other candidates have similar appeal. Approval voting would remove the justification for the current state laws that make it extremely difficult for third-party candidates to gain ballot access.

The split-vote problem is not a problem for corporate supporters; it is an opportunity that provides the legal basis for corporate supporters to enact laws that make ballot access extremely challenging—in some cases, virtually impossible— for third-party candidates. Gaining ballot access for third-party candidates is often prohibitively expensive. The political parties' elected officials, in order to protect their control of the political playing field, have passed a variety of very restrictive ballot access laws at the state level. These laws have proven to be effective in limiting those who can run for office and in preventing third-party candidates from being heard. The courts have upheld these laws on the basis that limiting the number of candidates to avoid the split-vote problem is desirable.

Using ballot access laws to control who can run for Congress or the presidency is inconsistent with our Constitution and the intent of the Founding Fathers. As Alexander Hamilton wrote in "Federalist No. 60":

> The truth is, that there is no method of securing to the rich the preference apprehended, but by prescribing qualifications of property either for those who may elect or be elected. But this forms no part of the power to be conferred upon the national government.

In its opinions, the Supreme Court has frequently quoted James Madison's statement during the Constitutional Convention debates: "A Republic may be converted into an aristocracy or oligarchy as well by limiting the number capable of being elected, as the number authorized to elect."

The two major parties control the state legislatures and Congress and thus control the process by which we elect members of Congress and the president. The Founding Fathers believed that having the right to vote—and thus having a say in who governs—is illusory if severe restrictions are in place vis-à-vis who can run for office.

Another problem is the great inconsistency in the states' ballot access laws. In some states it is virtually impossible to get on the ballot to run for Congress as a third-party candidate. The Supreme Court has recognized that there should be uniformity in qualifications for elected federal officials, and that these qualifications should be minimal. In its opinion in *US Term Limits, Inc. v. Thornton*, the Supreme Court quoted the opinion of Federal Appeals Court Judge Robert L. Brown:

> If there is one watchword for representation of the various states in Congress, it is uniformity. Federal legislators speak to national issues that affect the citizens of every state...Piecemeal restrictions by States would fly in the face of that order...

And also from the debates on the ratification of the Constitution:

> It has ever been considered a great security to liberty, that very few should be excluded from the right of being chosen to the legislature.

Unfortunately, ballot access laws lack uniformity, which frustrates the efforts of the people to exercise their right to choose their elected officials. These restrictive, heterogeneous ballot access laws take the sovereignty away from the people to freely choose their representatives to the national government. That "great security to liberty, that very few should be excluded from being chosen" that Justice Stevens noted no longer exists.

States' ballot access laws effectively limit the number of candidates who can gain ballot access. The right to vote is seriously undermined by such limitations. In the words of Justice Douglas, "...[T]the right to vote would be empty if the State could arbitrarily deny the right to stand for election." *Lubin v Panish* (1974).

On June 29, 1990, President George H. W. Bush signed the Copenhagen Document of the Organization for Security and Co-operation in Europe (OSCE), which states that signatories should:

> (7.5)—Respect the right of citizens to seek political or public office, individually or as representatives of political parties or organizations, without discrimination;
>
> (7.6)—Respect the right of individuals and groups to establish, in full freedom, their own political parties or other political organizations and provide such political parties and organizations with the necessary legal guarantees to enable them to compete with each other on a basis of equal treatment before the law and by the authorities…

The United States has been criticized for restrictive ballot access laws that are inconsistent with the agreement. National ballot access laws are the norm in other advanced countries.

During the 2004 presidential election, the Democrats worked to keep Ralph Nader off the ballot in every state; in 2012, Mitt Romney's Republican Party team worked to keep the Libertarian candidate, Gary Johnson, off state ballots, since they felt that Johnson would take away more Republican votes than Democratic votes. The Libertarian website, www .lp.org, stated on October 12, 2012:

Commonwealth Court Senior Judge James G. Colins ruled late today that the Libertarian Party of Pennsylvania...will remain on the November 6 general election ballot, including Libertarian two-term Governor Gary Johnson for President...The ruling was a stinging defeat for Republicans who waged a grueling and expensive 9-week battle to force their Libertarian Party competition off the November ballot...

Governor Johnson said, "It is a travesty of the democratic process that Libertarians were required to endure such a drawn-out, expensive and unnecessary attack on their right to be on the ballot...

LPPA Chairman of Dr. Tom Stevens, commented: We stood up to the superior resources of the Republican Party...faced with the possibility of a significant assessment of costs, sanctions and attorney's fees if we lost.

Restricting ballot access is one of the many tools that corporate agenda supporters have used in their consistent, pervasive, and effective efforts to nullify democracy.

To paraphrase James Madison speaking at the Constitutional Convention, we must prevent our republic from being converted into an aristocracy or oligarchy by limiting the number of people who are capable of being elected. Amending the Constitution to adopt approval voting and to require uniform and fair ballot access laws are essential steps to free us from the oligarchy's control of the electoral process. Allowing noncorporate supporters to join the campaign conversation, allowing voters to effectively express their concerns by enabling them to vote for candidates who speak to their concerns, and giving noncorporate supporter candidates a fair chance to gain support (and to have their voter support honestly recorded) are all essential steps in removing the corrupting influences that currently plague our democracy.

Section 3: Presidential Debates

An independent Presidential Debate Board (PDB), appointed by the president and approved of by the Senate, will plan the presidential debates and will decide the number of debates, as well as their format and location and who does the questioning. If the PDB manages a political party's primary debates and the winning candidate achieves a specified level of voter support as set by Congress, the winning candidate will be assured ballot access in all states and the right to participate in the presidential debates. The aforementioned Presidential Debate Board will be subject to a recall vote at the time of the presidential election; if recalled, a new board will be appointed in its place.

Reasons for Section 3

How did the Commission on Presidential Debates (CPD) come into existence? The name gives the commission an air of legitimacy, but that is the total substance of its legitimacy. The following is descriptive of the birth and functioning of the CPD:

OUR MISSION

The Commission on Presidential Debates (CPD) was established in 1987 to ensure that debates, as a permanent part of every general election, provide the best possible information to viewers and listeners. Its primary purpose is to sponsor and produce debates for the United States presidential and vice presidential candidates and to undertake research and educational activities relating to the debates. The organization, which is a nonprofit, nonpartisan, 501(c)(3) corporation, sponsored all the presidential debates in 1988, 1992, 1996, 2000, 2004, 2008, and 2012.

From 1960 until 1984 (before the birth of the CDP), the nonpartisan League of Women Voters (LWV) was in charge of the presidential debates. The league worked to ensure that the debates provided the best possible information to viewers and listeners. The LWV withdrew from the position as debate organizers in 1987 in protest of the Democratic and Republican party candidates' attempts to dictate nearly every aspect of the debates. On October 2, 1988, the LWV's fourteen trustees voted unanimously to pull out of the debates; the following news release was issued the next day in Washington, D.C.:

"The League of Women Voters is withdrawing its sponsorship of the presidential debate scheduled for mid-October because the demands of the two campaign organizations would perpetrate a fraud on the American voter," League President Nancy M. Neuman said today.

"It has become clear to us that the candidates' organizations aim to add debates to their list of campaign-trail charades devoid of substance, spontaneity and honest answers to tough questions," Neuman said. "The League has no intention of becoming an accessory to the hoodwinking of the American public."

Neuman said that the campaigns presented the League with their debate agreement on September 28, two weeks before the scheduled debate...[and] most objectionable to the League...were conditions in the agreement that gave the campaigns unprecedented control over the proceedings.

The citizenry needs to take control of the political conversation that leads to choosing the congressional members and the president. The public needs to move from controlled questioning of candidates and paid-for "free speech" by the plutocracy to questioning and discussions that would help voters understand the challenges the country faces and the candidates' proposals for dealing with them. Voters need the opportunity to vote based on good information and to choose from a broader choice of candidates. The news release continued by stating that Neuman and the LWV regretted that the people lacked real opportunities to judge presidential nominees outside of campaign-controlled environments; Neuman stated:

On the threshold of a new millennium, this country remains the brightest hope for all who cherish free speech and open debate...Americans deserve to see and hear the men who would be president face each other in a debate on the hard and complex issues critical to our progress into the next century. [She challenged the candidates to] rise above your handlers and agree to join us in presenting the fair and full discussion the American public expects of a League of Women Voters debate.

The candidates did not "rise above their handlers," however; control of the political discourse was and remains firmly in the hands of the plutocracy: their political handlers. The plutocracy has expended a great deal of effort and has consistently invested large sums of money to maintain and enhance its control of political discourse and the political process. This has been a very profitable investment by the plutocracy that has come at the expense of the "99 percent."

The CBD's polling requirements make it extremely difficult for third-party candidates to participate in the debates. Third-party candidates have to have at least 15 percent support across five national polls before they can participate in the debates. The problem here is that most third-party candidates face grave difficulties in attaining corporate media coverage and raising money beyond what they may acquire from small donors. The usual question asked in these polls is not, "Do you want the third-party candidate to participate in the debates?" but rather, "Who do you intend to vote for?" Most voters are not willing to indicate that they would vote for a third-party candidate who has had minimal coverage by the corporate media, as that would seem to be a "wasted" vote. Candidates' poll numbers do not fairly reflect their support. The system is rigged to make it virtually impossible for third-party candidates to be heard broadly on different issues, and to have a fair chance of participating in campaigns.

Not only are third-party candidates denied access to the debates and fair coverage, the debates do not allow for any real vetting of the main political party candidates, who do not face any serious questioning about their proposed programs and policies, their avoidance of serious issues, and their implied assumptions about what would be best for the United States. Candidates will often assert, when justifying proposed American foreign policy or actions abroad, that these actions will protect American interests, with no mention of what those interests are—as if ordinary citizens do not need to know what those interests are and whose interests they are.

During a 2008 primary debate between Hillary Clinton and Barack Obama, moderated by George Stephanopoulos and Charlie Gibson *of ABC News*, the moderators failed to ask one serious question during the first fifty-three minutes of the debate. At times, the primary debates appear like a professional wrestling match: where the winner is not the issue, it's the show that matters, and no one gets hurt.

The following is an open letter signed by forty journalists and published in the blog *The Economist's View* following that debate:

We the undersigned deplore the conduct of ABC's George Stephanopoulos and Charles Gibson at the Democratic presidential debate on April 16, 2008...

For 53 minutes, we heard no question about public policy from either moderator…Many thousands of those viewers have already written to ABC to express their outrage…We're at a crucial moment in our country's history, facing war, a terrorism threat, recession, and a range of big domestic challenges. Large majorities of our fellow Americans tell pollsters they're deeply worried about the country's direction. In such a context, journalists moderating a debate—who are, after all, entrusted with free public airwaves—have a particular responsibility to push and engage the candidates in serious debate about these matters…In the words of Tom Shales of the *Washington Post*, Mr. Gibson and Mr. Stephanopoulos turned in "shoddy, despicable performances." As Greg Mitchell of *Editor and Publisher* describes it, the debate was a "travesty." We hope that the public uproar over ABC's miserable showing will encourage a return to serious journalism in debates.

During the 2012 Republican primary debates, virtually none of the candidates (with the exception of Ron Paul) engaged in any in-depth discussions about the serious challenges that faced the nation. Paul was a Libertarian candidate who ran as a Republican because he believed that would afford him the opportunity to be heard by a national audience. Since the Republican party bosses controlled the Republican primary debates, Paul was not given a fair chance to participate in the debates. (This situation will be discussed in detail in the discussion of Section.5.)

The Republican primary debate and the presidential debates in 2012 were a continuation of the charade, and were devoid of real substance. Viewers heard proclamations being made without any supporting explanations: repeal "Obamacare," repeal Dodd-Frank (i.e., the Dodd-Frank Wall Street Reform and Consumer Protection Act), reinstate the Bush tax cuts, cut entitlements. The polices that the candidates put forth were very similar to those of the George W. Bush years (2000–2008), with no critique of how well those policies worked and no deliberate mentioning of the second Bush presidency. It was as if that presidency had not happened; instead, we were to repeat many of the same policies, with no accountability.

While many Democratic voters during the 2012 election were disappointed with the Obama presidency, during the primary debate season, these voters would not hear a critique of his performance in office, nor would they have the opportunity to have a spokesperson for their concerns or to express their disappointment by voting for an alternative choice. During the primaries, Democratic primary voters did not have the opportunity to hold President Obama accountable for his performance in office. The Democrats also did not want (nor would they advocate for) an open and honest critique of Obama's performance, since that would have threatened his incumbency, it would have implied that politicians should be held accountable for their actions in office, and it would have threatened corporate interests. Holding corporate protectors accountable for serving the corporate interests is taboo in the current political theater, and is religiously followed by Democrats and Republicans alike—arguably more so for the Democrats.

We need the opportunity to challenge incumbent presidents and to have the opportunity to debate them during the primaries. The political parties make it virtually impossible to challenge a president who is running for reelection in the party primaries. A challenge would be considered a disloyal political move that would not be supported by the political party; the party officials would say that such a challenge ignores what is best for the country. The President is the top political party boss and, with very few exceptions, no challengers or primary debates take place for a political party that has an incumbent president in office. There is, however, ample opportunity for praise and applause and the waving of flags.

The political polls showed that the public had grave concerns about major issues during the Bush (2004) and Obama (2012) administrations. Nevertheless, no questioning was done within the Republican Party in 2004 for the failure of intelligence in preventing the September 11 terrorist attacks or in taking the country to war in Iraq after false claims had been made of a clear and present danger of weapons of mass destruction (WMDs). In 2012, the polls showed that the Democratic Party had grave concerns about President

Obama's handling of the banking bailout and many other important issues. During the 2012 general election, the candidates made many claims without being seriously questioned and made proclamations without supporting evidence; they continued to avoid many issues of great concern to a majority of voters, and made uncontested proclamations such as "I will create twelve million jobs" and "No bankers broke the laws." We need tough questioning with adequate time allowed for meaningful answers, and an insistence that the question asked is the question answered during follow-up questions.

Taking the primary debates out of the control of the political party bosses (the president being the top boss) would allow primary challengers to engage an incumbent president in real discussions of the president's policies, programs, and his/her performance in office. Hearing these discussions, voters during the primaries could have a meaningful say in deciding the candidate selection that would determine whether or not the president should be the party's candidate.

John Kellett & Christine Kellett

Section 4: Independent Parties and Independent Voters' Primaries

The Presidential Debate Board (PDB) will manage an Independent Voters' Primary debate process leading up to the primary elections. Every state shall hold an independent voters' primary for president; every political party that has achieved a specified level of support (to be set by Congress) and that has abided by the rules of the PDB shall be entitled to place a candidate or candidates on the independent voters' primary ballot.

The winner of the independent voters' primary election, and any other candidate who receives a specified level of support (to be set by Congress) in the primaries, shall be entitled to appear on all state ballots and to participate in the presidential debates.

Reasons for Section 4

As noted above, Justice Souter, delivering the opinion of the Supreme Court in *Norman v. Reed* (1992), stated:

> For more than two decades, this Court has recognized the constitutional right of citizens to create and develop new political parties. The right ... advances the constitutional interest of likeminded voters to gather in pursuit of common political ends, thus enlarging the opportunities of all voters to express their own political preferences.

More voters are registered as Independents than there are voters registered as either Democrats or Republicans. These voters do not want to be identified as either Democrat or Republican. Polls have often indicated that a majority of the voters would like to have another candidate in the race because the voters are not happy with either the Republican or the Democrat on the ticket. In the 2012 presidential race between Romney and Obama, for example, in some swing states more than 90 percent of the political ads were negative, the message being variations on "Vote for me because my opponent is so awful." Voting is devalued if the voters do not have the option of voting for a candidate who speaks to their concerns. Voting for a candidate primarily as a way of defeating the candidate whom one dislikes most—and voting for this candidate primarily because he or she may defeat an even greater perceived evil—is not indicative of a healthy democracy. Voters need more options if real discussions of the issues are going to be part of the vetting process, and to assure that a candidate's chief loyalty lies with the voters and the United States as a whole, and not to the Democratic or Republican Party and their respective financial backers.

If citizens are to be able to exercise their constitutional right "to create and develop new political parties," as Justice Souter put it, third-party candidates need an equal opportunity to be on the ballots (in all fifty states) alongside the candidates of the major political parties. They need a fair chance to participate in the presidential debates, and the opportunity to be heard and have media coverage before the general election campaign: coverage that goes beyond answering the question, "Why are you running as a spoiler candidate?"

As was emphasized earlier, both ballot access and participation in the presidential debates are controlled by the Republicans and Democratic parties, with the essential financial support provided by the corporate-interest protectors. Republican and Democratic officials have determined the rules that govern ballot access and those that determine participation in the presidential debates in a manner that deliberately and severely disadvantages third-party candidates. Judges who have been appointed by either the Republicans or the Democrats have effectively prevented like-minded voters from, as Justice Souter termed it, "gathering in pursuit of common political ends" by preventing any effective appeal of different states' ballot access laws. This is an indirect form of voter suppression: preventing voters from expressing their concerns with their vote.

In the 1850s, the two main political parties, the Whigs and the Democrats, did not discuss the burning issue of the day—slavery—in any meaningful way. The Whigs and the Democrats' failure to discuss this issue resulted in the birth of the Republican Party. The Republican Party candidates took a stand on the slavery question. In 1858, Abraham Lincoln ran as a Republican against Stephen A. Douglas of the Democratic Party, the incumbent US Senator for Illinois. Lincoln was able to gain national recognition as a result of the famous Lincoln-Douglas debates. These represented meaningful debates between a third-party candidate and a political leader of one of the two main political parties. At that time, the voters voted for the political party, and not the candidates directly. The debates allowed Lincoln to lead the Republican Party to win the popular vote in the election in Illinois. However, US senators were appointed by the state legislators at that time, and the Democrats, helped by reapportionment of congressional districts, retained control of the legislature, which resulted in Douglas being re-appointed as senator. After the election, Lincoln wrote to a friend, "I am glad I made the late race…It gave me a hearing on the great and durable question of the age, which I could not have had in any other way…I believe I have made some marks that will tell for the cause of civil liberty long after I am gone." A poor lawyer, and a third-party candidate at that, speaking out against the vested interests in today's electoral process would have an extremely difficult time "making some marks" that would leave a mark long after he or she was gone.

The independent voters' primary would provide an opportunity for third-party voices to be heard, and for the issues they raise to get media coverage—coverage that they are not getting at the moment. This is the free speech that is essential to the health of our democracy. The nation faces a variety of challenges that are barely addressed by the Democratic and Republican candidates, who address virtually all of these challenges with carefully considered constraints so that the options they put forward are ones that will not unduly affect corporations' interests. Third-party candidates are third-party candidates most often because they are not wearing corporate-interest blinders. They have different ways of seeing and addressing the challenges that face the nation. Their participation in the primaries would allow significant challenges to be discussed, and would make room for proposals for meeting these challenges that differ from the options that are currently considered.

Citizens need to have the opportunity to show support for the candidates they feel propose governmental programs they support, even if they know these candidates have very little chance of winning. Support for a third-party candidate can form the basis for an effective lobbying group and for building support in future elections. With the adoption of approval voting, a general presidential race with more than two candidates would not result in the split-vote problem: as we've discussed, the distortion in the measuring of candidate support.

Requiring the states to hold independent voters' primaries would ensure uniformity of the process for third-party candidates to run for president. The independent voters' primaries would ensure the nomination of at least one third-party candidate who would be on the ballot and participate in the presidential debates. Such a system would prevent the corporate-interest protectors from narrowing the race to the two who are chosen from the major political parties: candidates who are funded by corporations, promoted by corporate media, and certified to be corporate-interest protectors. A third-party candidate who meaningfully participates in a general presidential election would make it considerably more difficult to narrow the field of topics to be discussed in the candidate-vetting process, and it would also prevent the Democratic or Republican candidates from limiting the range of the discussion on given topics. This would encourage meaningful citizen participation and would provide better opportunities for disseminating information regarding the candidates and their party platforms.

The independent primary would assure that at least one third-party candidate will have ballot access and be able to take part in the presidential debates; approval voting will assure that the voters can express their concerns by their votes, and that those votes will be an honest indicator of candidate support; and the proposed PDB will assure that all candidates will have a fair chance to discuss important issues in the presidential debates. Working together, these three reforms will result in a broad and honest vetting of the candidates.

Section 5: Media Oversight

(5a) In any presidential election year, public media will spend a significant amount of time interviewing presidential candidates and covering pertinent national issues. A Public Media Board (PMB) appointed by the president and approved of by the Senate will select independent groups to lead discussions on public media and on government-purchased time on other media.

(5b) In the general presidential election campaign, the PMB will partially fund private media so that candidates who are on all of the state ballots will have considerable opportunities to discuss national issues. The PMB will be adequately funded by the federal government. The PMB will be subject to a recall vote at the time of the presidential election; if recalled, a new board will be appointed.

Reasons for Section 5(a)

This and the previous section of the VRA are major steps in taking control of the election "sound system" from the plutocracy. The reform of ballot access and the expanded primary system will allow candidates to get to the microphone. This section of the amendment will assure that all candidates have a fair opportunity for mainstream media coverage. Corporate-supported candidates will have to compete in a noncorporate-controlled environment—in an actual marketplace of ideas.

These discussions during the presidential campaign will provide candidates with an opportunity to gain support based on their stances on issues—thus removing the need for massive financial backing from the plutocracy in order to gain support that is based primarily on "noise."

Voices that call for accountability, that speak out about corporate greed, that question statements that serve corporate interests are not meaningfully heard in the presidential selection process. Protecting corporate interests has been the guiding principle in the shaping of election noise.

Advocating for military expenditures and the support of wars to protect "our interests," without any clarification of what those interests might be, is an important step in gaining corporate media coverage and corporate support. Questioning the wisdom or motives for a war does not gain a candidate coverage; it raises questions about the viability of a candidate's political campaign, and it removes any chance of fair coverage of his or her campaign by the corporate media.

Mitt Romney, as a presidential candidate during the 2012 race, used the code phrases of a corporate supporter and gained massive financial backing from corporate-interest protectors as a result. During a presidential debate on June 13, 2011, Romney said:

> I think we've learned some important lessons in our experience in Afghanistan. I want those troops to come home based upon not politics, not based upon economics, but instead based upon the conditions on the ground determined by the generals.

Ignore the cost, ignore the broad political consequences of fighting wars, and just ask the generals what we should do?

John Kellett & Christine Kellett

These statements are assurances to the corporate supporters that the candidate can be counted on to be supportive of wars and military expenditures; they are code for "I am a supporter." Not to be outdone, candidate Tim Pawlenty replied in the debate with the following:

> Senator Biden has been wrong about every major strategic decision in the modern history of the international conflict and military. Look at his judgment about partitioning Iraq, for example. Now we have Iraq being probably one of the shining examples of success in the Middle East.

Even the promoters of the war in Iraq would have a difficult time saying that it was a "shining example of success in the Middle East." Only the aforementioned Libertarian candidate, Ron Paul (campaigning as a Republican), questioned that statement, and his remarks were kept to a minimum by the corporate-protector moderators and were not discussed further by the mainstream media. Paul was the only Democratic or Republican candidate in the 2012 presidential race to show a disposition for making statements that challenged the corporate interests. Paul said in the debates:

> I tell the generals what to do…I'd start taking care of people here at home because we could save hundreds of billions of dollars. Our national security is not enhanced by our presence over there. We have

no purpose there. We should learn the lessons of history...We spend $1.5 trillion overseas in wars that we don't need to be in and we need to cut there...and then put this money back into our economy here.

The carefully selected conservative audiences always applauded loudly when Paul made foreign policy statements about stopping the wars and cutting these expenditures. However, after the second Republican debate, the Republican debate moderators managed to steer almost completely clear of any questions for him that would allow him to make his foreign policy positions clear; they also asked Romney and Texas Governor Rick Perry far more questions than they asked Paul.

The examples of the media coverage of Ron Paul's candidacy during the 2012 Republican primary are representative of the corporate media coverage of noncorporate protectors who get a microphone—those who pretend to be a Democrat or a Republican so that they can get to a microphone that will have an audience.

When the mainstream corporate media covered Paul's comments, which was not often, it would avoid his anticorporate interest concerns; instead, the media referred to parts of his monetary policy that did not have wide public support or to statements he had made concerning social policies. The following quotes are from newspaper articles; these were the only references to Paul in the respective articles. These are typical of the mainstream media coverage.

Charles Lane wrote in The *Washington Post*, September 9, 2011,

> Ron Paul and his supporters gripe that the media do not give his campaign the attention it deserves. OK, let's focus on his animadversions in Wednesday night's Republican debate. He seemed to advocate a new system of silver coinage, just like the one we had in the eighteenth century...according to Gallup, Paul is in a statistical dead heat with President Obama. That's right: When it comes to their choice for president in 2012, Americans are equally divided between the incumbent and this rambling, ultra-libertarian gold bug. This must be a measurement of Obama's political weakness, because it cannot possibly reflect widespread support for Paul's loopy ideas.

According to the *Post*, it was clearly not worth discussing the unfavorable antiwar "animadversion" statements of this "rambling, ultra-libertarian gold bug," as he only had "loopy ideas." The following are examples of Paul's Republican primary debate statements that the media did not discuss.

> May 5, 2011: Well I think strength is good, but you have to have strength in doing the right things. I think secret military prisons, keeping people there for years and years without due process, is not characteristic of a republic that believes in freedom. It's more typical of an authoritarian government to have secret prisons. So therefore I don't think it serves our purpose.

September 5, 2011: Well, I would take the advice of the Founders and I would take the advice of George Bush when he ran in the year 2000—no nation-building. You know, don't go be the policemen of the world.

Mike Littwin wrote in the *Denver Post* on September 8, 2011:

If you watched the debate, you saw that co-moderator Brian Williams knows enough about good TV to make this into a Perry-Romney affair. They stood in the middle of the crowd of eight candidates, side by side, one often staring at the other. Except for the odd Ron Paul moment—and there were a few—it wasn't always obvious anyone else was on the stage.

Brian Williams "knew enough" about good TV to make this into a Perry-Romney affair, and the mainstream media declared Perry to be a top-tier candidate. Yet Perry's total vote count in the primaries was less than fifty-five thousand, while Paul's total primary vote exceeded two million. Perry did not come close to receiving more votes than Paul in any single primary.

A "Ron Paul moment" clearly is not meant as a compliment; this was the substance of the Paul coverage. A statement from Paul in the September 7, 2011 debate follows; we can surmise that this is a "Ron Paul moment":

I strongly supported Ronald Reagan. I was one of four in Texas—one of four members of Congress that supported Reagan in '76. And I supported him all along, and I supported his—his—all his issues and all his programs. But in the 1980s, we spent too much, we taxed too much, we built up our deficits, and it was a bad scene. Therefore, I support the message of Ronald Reagan. The message was great. But the consequence, we have to be honest with ourselves. It was not all that great.

Nate Silver wrote in the *New York Times*, September 9, 2011:

I've developed a habit—it's probably a bad habit—of assigning letter grades to the Republican candidates based on my initial reaction to their performance in debates. After Wednesday night's debate in Simi Valley, I gave Rick Perry a B-minus, meaning an average performance. Meanwhile, I gave Mitt Romney, his primary rival for the Republican nomination, a higher grade of A-minus.

The grades are based on neither style nor substance per se, but instead mostly on strategy: how much each candidate did to improve his chances of winning the nomination.

Media coverage of the debates is primarily about the contest rather than about the issues that were discussed and the issues the candidates failed to discuss, or the legitimacy or importance of the candidates' statements. Note that the race as described is between Perry and Romney; Paul is not mentioned in the

Times article. Paul always led Perry in the polls and received significantly more votes in every contest that they both participated in.

The corporate media's treatment of Paul in the 2012 primaries is the way that noncorporate supporters are covered. As the *Chicago Tribune* wrote on September 8, 2011, "there was little sign that Rep. Ron Paul of Texas, who continues to fare well in some polls, was any closer to breaking out as a mainstream threat." What does it mean "to break out as a mainstream threat"? The candidates who are portrayed as not "breaking out as a mainstream threat" and projected as not doing well in the voting are the noncorporate supporter candidates. Google "media blackout of Ron Paul" to get a quick view of the TV coverage of Ron Paul.

As of this writing (2016), Senator Bernie Sanders of Vermont is running for president. He ran and won his senate race as an Independent. Like Rep. Ron Paul in 2012, Senator Sanders is running on a major party ticket (as a Democrat) so that he stands a chance of having a national audience. If Senator Sanders had run for president as an Independent, where he would be supported by his political party, he would have had virtually no national coverage, and thus no opportunity to participate in the presidential debates.

Like Ron Paul in the 2012 race, Bernie Sanders discusses issues that are antagonistic to the plutocracy's interests. The corporate media did not fairly characterize Ron Paul on the issues during the 2012 race, and many in the media have characterized Sanders as just another Ron Paul. Typical of the coverage of Sander's presidential campaign is the July 7, 2015, front page of the *New York Times*: a thirty-five-column-inch article in which thirty-three column inches cover the effect that Sanders's presence in the campaign has had on Hillary Clinton's campaign. On the inside page, two column inches cover Sanders's appeal, based on issues. In these two column inches, the *Times* states that Sanders wants to spend a trillion dollars on infrastructure and advocates a massive tax increase. There is no clarification of the time span of spending that trillion dollars, or of whose taxes would be increased and by how much; this is typical of the coverage of Sanders's campaign and the issues he raises.

All too often the race-who is winning or losing- is the content of the coverage, with the light shining on the corporate supporters or coverage that is just a distraction away from substantive issues. The coverage of Donald Trump has high distraction value, and distractions are important when there is a Sanders's campaign against corporate control to be aggressively ignored. The goal here is fair coverage of the issues Sanders, or any other candidate, raises.

The treatment of third-party candidates raises a question that is similar to the question that philosophers ask: "If a tree falls in the forest and nobody is around to hear it, does it make a sound?" If a candidate makes a speech and he or she is not heard by a critical mass of citizens and the speech is not covered by the media, has that candidate made a speech? Just as the coverage of third party candidates is minimal, the coverage of the issues they raise is virtually nonexistent.

On December 13, 2011, Rocky Anderson, former mayor of Salt Lake City and a former Democrat, announced his candidacy for president and the formation of a new political party called the Justice Party. There would be virtually no coverage of the Justice Party or of Anderson's candidacy by the corporate mainstream media. Anderson provided a critique of Obama's presidency that consisted of attacks on the president's protection of the plutocracy's interests. His criticism differed substantially from what was heard from the Republican candidates' critiques of Obama's performance in office. And, because there were no Democratic candidates to critique Obama's performance, this critique was missing from the 2012 campaign coverage that the public heard. The following is a partial statement of Anderson's critique.

Well, President Obama would like us to ignore what's happened these past four years. And granted, he came into a tough situation, but we have to consider that during the last forty-three months we've had more than eight percent unemployment…The fact is that in the downturn, sixty percent of the jobs lost were mid-skill and midpaying jobs, and only twenty percent of the new jobs during the so-called recovery are of that category, the midskill and midpaying jobs. Most of the jobs are low-paying jobs. These new jobs that he brags about, they're in retail sales and in food preparation…

We need to renegotiate the outrageous free trade agreements and make sure they are fair trade, so that we're not discriminating against those employers who want to hire United States workers. And also we need to get a handle on healthcare costs, because there are a tremendous competitive disadvantages because of the cost of healthcare in this country. The solution to Medicare is to provide Medicare for everybody, to make it a single-payer system. If you look around the world—Canada, Taiwan—Taiwan did a study. They looked at all other nations' systems, and they incorporated the very best elements. And they have a single-payer, basically Medicare-for-all system…

As to Social Security, the Social Security payroll tax is as regressive a tax known to mankind, because if you make over $110,000, you don't pay anything on the income over that amount. Everybody pays the same thing up to that point. We need to lift that cap. You could reduce the percentage that workers pay. You could bring it down to four percent, so that the middle class and the working poor come out ahead. You lift the cap, and then you also have those who make their money through investments pay their fair share, as well.

Similarly, the issues raised by Dr. Jill Stein, the Green Party presidential candidate, were not to be covered by the mainstream media.

Taking control of the "sound system" takes the vetting process for presidential candidates out of the hands of the political party bosses, and thus out of the control of the plutocracy. The proposed Public Media Board's influence on the vetting process and the coverage of the vetting process would force a broader, more complete, and better reported discussion of national issues by all candidates—and not the very carefully tailored discussion of a limited selection of topics by corporate protectors.

Reasons for Section 5(b)

The goal of this part of the amendment is to reduce the role of money in politics by decreasing the role of campaign financing in managing an effective presidential campaign. The focus is on campaign reform, and not simply campaign finance reform. Reforming political campaigns depends on providing adequate funding for an adequate amount of time on the airwaves for the candidates to have in-depth discussions of the challenges that face the nation, and adequate time to critique or defend existing policies or programs and the administration of those policies or programs. This would allow vetting of the candidates based on free speech, not the speech that is bought and paid for by sixty-second corporate "free speech"—the free speech for which a candidate has to be grateful to his or her corporate sponsors for providing funding; the free speech that the corporate-interest protectors on the Supreme Court, in the *Citizens United* case, ruled to be constitutionally protected speech; the "free speech" for which it is not sufficient to say "thank you" to the corporate sponsors. Candidates are expected to express gratitude, and they must act to protect the corporate interests by word and deed: persistently, consistently, and without significant deviation from the protectors' script.

Over 2.5 billion dollars were spent during the 2012 presidential election campaign: that is a lot of money that the political party candidates had to express gratitude for. This figure represents more than twice the amount spent during the 2008 presidential campaign—an increase that was made possible by the *Citizens United* case. *Citizens United* released corporate free speech from the control of federal laws. That money paid for a lot of free speech in which no major national issues were discussed; a lot of major questions that were of great concern to a significant percentage of citizens were effectively and completely ignored by the candidates from the main political parties.

Below are some of the questions that the corporate protectors did not want to be asked (or answered) during the 2012 presidential election that were avoided by the top-tier candidates, and that the polls indicated the public wanted to see addressed:

- Are corporations persons?
- Is the rapid widening of the distribution of income desirable?
- Should we have a single-payer health care system?
- Should it be illegal for citizens to buy drugs in foreign countries that are identical to those available in the United States as a way to save money?
- Should the government negotiate drug prices when it pays the bill with taxpayers' dollars?

- What do we hope to accomplish by staying in Afghanistan, what are we likely to accomplish, and is it worth the additional cost?
- Why do we allow banks that are too big to fail to continue to exist?
- Why did we allow large bonuses to be paid to bankers when we were using taxpayers' dollars to bail banks out as a result of fraudulent banking practices?
- Why were no bankers prosecuted for knowingly selling fraudulent financial securities?
- Does our spending more money on the military than all other nations combined enhance our security?
- When people say that "we are protecting American interests" by our various military involvements, what (or whose) interests are they talking about?
- What are the risks of global warming? Should we have policies in place that reduce those risks?
- Why do we have more people in prison per capita than any other nation?
- Have we negotiated any international trade agreements that have hurt the job opportunities in the United States?
- Why does the government allow mergers that result in a few corporations controlling a large segment of the economy, with virtually no discussion of the impact of these mergers on communities, jobs, the economy, the environment, the work environment, the retirement promised to workers, the desirability of the new

jobs, the creativity of the work force, the ability of government to regulate corporations, and on and on?

Third-party candidates raised these issues, but third-party candidates' discussions were not heard.

Redefining the nature of the presidential campaign is essential. Campaigns should not be forced to spend huge sums of money to pay for "robocalls." Instead, we should take steps to make significant amounts of TV time available to all candidates for in-depth discussions of important national issues. This would open the marketplace of political ideas to real ideas, thus making it a competitive marketplace: this is centrally important in the vetting of candidates for elected, federal office. The control of the election sound system could be taken out of the hands of the corporate protectors by doing the following:

- The expanded independent primary would provide a real path for noncorporate candidates to participate in the presidential race as candidates who are actually aligned with their true political party affiliations.
- The creation of the proposed Presidential Debate Board would take the debates out of the hands of the Republican and Democratic political party bosses.
- The creation of the proposed Public Media Board would assure that significant mainstream media time would be available for in-depth discussions of a broad spectrum of important national issues.

- Changing to an approval voting system would allow voters to show their support for candidates who address their concerns.

Third-party candidates and the main political parties' candidates all deserve fair mainstream media coverage of the issues they raise, as well as coverage and discussion of the important issues they avoid. Good discussions of important issues are essential to meaningful involvement in the political process. Promoting voter involvement that goes beyond supporting a candidate because he or she is the Democratic or Republican candidate: or, as is so often the case, supporting the Republican candidates because they are not the Democratic candidate, or supporting the Democratic candidates because they are not the Republican candidate. Real involvement, upon which the health of our democracy depends, means being able to actively support a candidate because that candidate identifies, clarifies, and supports policies and programs that you would like to support; such candidates give you reason to believe that they will strive for the real change they promise.

Section 6: Recounts

During presidential elections, a presidential candidate may challenge the counting in any five congressional districts and acquire a supervised recount. If the count is substantially inaccurate, the count will not be considered to be one of the challenges.

Reasons for Section 6

Votes should be counted and, if necessary, undergo a federally supervised recount during federal elections. Elections should not be decided by five members of the Supreme Court as in the 2000*Bush v. Gore* decision, which was a five-to-four decision. Bush was declared the winner in Florida by less than six hundred votes, even though over sixty thousand votes were in question. If any one of those five majority justices had decided that the people's vote should decide the election, then the votes would have been counted and the people would have decided the election. It appears that the corporate-interest protectors on the Supreme Court need special guidance on how the democratic process is supposed to work.

The US Supreme Court put an injunction on the Florida recount after the Florida Supreme Court had ordered that the recount should proceed. When Justice Scalia was asked why the Supreme Court stopped the recount, he replied that the court stopped the recount to "protect the ballots." More recently, Justice Scalia was asked about the *Bush v. Gore* decision in an interview, and he replied that it came down to who should make the decision—the Florida Supreme Court or the US Supreme Court—and he felt that it should be the latter.

That fundamentally misstates the situation, since the Florida Supreme Court, consistent with all previous laws and traditions, had directed that the election should not be decided by the court, but rather by the people counting the votes: in other words, by the universally accepted procedure in healthy democracies. Justice Stevens wrote in his dissent to *Bush v. Gore* (2000):

> Time will one day heal the wound to that confidence that will be inflicted by today's decision. One thing, however, is certain. Although we may never know with complete certainty the identity of the winner of this year's Presidential election, the identity of the loser is perfectly clear. It is the Nation's confidence in the judge as an impartial guardian of the rule of law. I respectfully dissent.

The constitutional amendment that protects the right to vote by disallowing a poll tax as a requirement to vote (Amendment XXIV), and the constitutional amendment that extends the right to vote to women (Amendment XIX), start with similar statements:

> The right of citizens of the United States to vote in any primary or other election for President or Vice President, for electors for President or Vice President, or for Senator or Representative in Congress, shall not be denied or abridged by the United States or any State...

> The right of citizens of the United States to vote shall not be denied or abridged by the United States or by any State...

The clear purpose of these amendments is to prevent the government from denying or abridging a citizen's right to vote. Preventing the counting of votes, or not assuring the honest counting of votes, constitutes denying and abridging the right to vote. The right of candidates and citizens to have their votes counted, and counted fairly, needs to be clearly, constitutionally protected.

It is essential that candidates, just like football coaches and tennis players, have the power to challenge the officials. Candidates should be able to challenge election officials when there is evidence of possible incorrect reporting of election results. The possibility of a challenge will be a deterrent to reporting wrong results, and will also allow for a remedy for any errors that are made. Our democracy is seriously impaired when votes are not counted, or when voting results are not reported honestly; citizens lose faith in the fairness of elections and the efficacy of voting when the votes are not counted, or are not counted fairly.

Section 7: Voting Records

Control of vote counting will be at the voting district level, and paper records will be kept for at least one year following elections.

Reasons for Section 7

Computer control of voting and counting the ballots allows for the possibility of large-scale fraud. The control of the voting system by one of the main political parties in each of the states brings into serious question the fairness of the process.

In December 2007, Ohio's Secretary of State, Jennifer Brunner, faulted the administration of Ohio's 2004 presidential voting. The computer servers for the Ohio vote count were in the same building in Chattanooga, Tennessee, as the computer servers for the Republican National Committee. Ken Blackwell, Ohio's Secretary of State in 2004, was the top election official at the time, as well as being co-chair of the Bush-Cheney campaign. Many of the election ballots were destroyed after the election, thus ensuring that an Ohio recount would be impossible.

In an interview on the news program *Democracy Now!*, Harvey Wasserman, author of *What Happened in Ohio: A Documentary Record of Theft and Fraud in the 2004 Election*, maintained that:

> We never got the slightest bit of help from the Democratic Party...The **biggest opposition** we got to pointing out that the 2004 election was stolen has

come from the Democrats, because—who knows? I
can't even begin to psychoanalyze them.

Neither political party is enthusiastic about holding officials
accountable for official acts. Holding public officials accountable can be contagious, spreading like a bad flu in winter, since
once such accountability is started, the other side will want
to retaliate. The accused party will also show that this kind
of behavior is not peculiar to their party. The code of ethical political behavior, well understood by both political parties' bosses, is that "this political party official is not to hold
other political party officials accountable for official acts."
Accountability gets in the way of supporting and promoting the corporate interests' agendas. Accountability jeopar-
dizes fund raising; threatens incumbency, as well as personal
and family money-making opportunities; and it weakens the
power of the elected office. And if the political parties do not
go after officials' sleight of hand, then both political parties
can abuse their power and can be abusive to third-party candidates, and nobody will be held accountable.

The Democratic Party officials are at least as faithful
to the doctrine of no accountability for official acts as the
Republicans are. That is not to say that private immorality
(as opposed to official, public-office wrongdoing) will not be
exposed, especially by the Republican Party officials. This
sort of accountability does not threaten the corporate interests, and it helps to project a sense that the political party
officials are moral people: officials who will not tolerate bad
behavior. The message to be sent out is that "Our party

officials want to exorcise those who are not God-fearing, moral-behaving, law-abiding, and publicly concerned officials; badly behaving officeholders have no place in the federal government." But correcting fraud in vote counting sends the wrong message: that elected officials sometimes behave badly in their official acts, and that the legitimacy of the electoral process is to be questioned.

Elected officials focus on voter fraud that results from voters voting illegally. While such fraud virtually never happens these days, this focus helps to project an image of concern for voter fraud. This focus on individual bad behavior —even if that behavior is imaginary— helps to provide cover for not addressing official fraud. This focus also becomes part of the distracting package of ideas that allows candidates to sound like they are saying something, when actually they are saying nothing about the most critical national challenges or national opportunities.

The real need is to focus on the illegitimate transfer of power as a result of not counting the votes or of erroneously counting the votes. The illegitimate holding or transferring of power is the most serious threat to democracy; it is often what undermines democracies—or even destroys them.

Section 8: The Electoral College

In presidential elections using approval voting, each candidate will be assigned electoral votes from each state in proportion to his/her voter support, rounded off to one decimal point. A candidate's voter support will be determined by dividing the number of votes each candidate receives by the total number of voters.

Reasons for Section 8
Under our present system of plurality voting, the state boss of the political party that is in the majority, whether Democratic or Republican, takes advantage of his or her majority position to maximize the party's political power, to minimize any recognition of minority parties, and to concentrate citizen voting power in the voters of his or her own party. To maximize their political clout during presidential elections, the bosses, with very few exceptions, have decided that the winner of the presidential election in their states will be assigned all of the electoral votes of that state, regardless of how close the vote count is. All other party candidates get a total of zero electoral votes.

In the 1992 presidential election, Bill Clinton got 42 percent of the popular vote and 68.8 percent of the electoral vote, George H. W. Bush got 37.5 percent of the popular vote and 31.2 percent of the electoral vote, and Ross Perot got 19 percent of the popular vote and 0 percent of the electoral votes. It is not at all clear who would have won if Perot had not been in the race. Clinton's electoral vote made him look like a big winner, but significantly less than a majority of the voters supported his election. In the 2000 election, Al Gore won the popular vote, but George W. Bush won the electoral vote—and thus the election. In the 2012 election, Obama had 51 percent of the popular vote and 62 percent of the electoral vote, while Romney had 48 percent of the popular vote and 38 percent of the electoral vote.

The electoral count determines the outcome of the presidential election. Thus, while the electoral vote gains the lion's share of the attention in reporting on the election results, the electoral vote distorts the candidates' support. Approval voting, and a proportional allocation of the electoral vote according to voter support, would assure that candidates' support is measured in a valid way, and that the assignment of electoral votes will not distort the level of that support.

The political decision to assign the electoral vote by the winner take all system during presidential general elections works to nullify the democratic process in several ways. First, it distorts the value of a vote, depending on the residency of a voter. In the three largest states, California, Texas, and New York, voters can be quite certain about which of the political party candidates is going to win all of the electoral votes from their state, even before the candidates are nominated. In these states, a majority of the voters vote for their political party's candidate, or they vote against the other political party's candidate, regardless of the candidate who is running. A person's vote in these states is essentially worthless—especially if one is a member of the minority party. Campaigning within the biggest states is not particularly meaningful, and thus considerably less campaigning takes place in the biggest states than in some of the medium and small swing states. Second, because of the winner take all system, striving to help a third-party candidate get his/her message out and gain support is extremely discouraging; most citizens understand this to be a waste of their efforts, since they will most certainly get zero electoral votes. This is true in the vast majority of states, because most subscribe to the winner take all system—there is little reason to campaign there or even to vote, as there is good reason to believe that your efforts will not matter.

If a voter lives in a swing state, however—a state that may go either way in the election—campaigning and getting out the vote for the candidate is critical for success. In the 2000 presidential election, six states were decided by fewer than eight thousand votes each. These six states have a total of fifty-nine electoral votes. In the 2000 election, a switch of three electoral votes would have changed the outcome. In the 2004 election, a switch of eighteen electoral votes (out of the total number of 712) would have changed the outcome. Consequently, small states that are also swing states can receive more attention than the more populous states, and votes in these states are more valuable than those of voters in one of the country's most populous states.

The proportional allocation of electoral votes according to voter support has several positive aspects when used in conjunction with approval voting:

- Approval voting allows for an honest measure of voter support for each of the candidates, and proportional allocation of electoral votes allows for an honest and fair allocation of electoral votes.

- Votes in different states will have approximately the same value, since every vote for a candidate contributes proportionally to the calculation of that candidate's electoral votes.

- Third-party candidates, by receiving an honest recording of support and the honest allocation of electoral votes, will have a fair chance to build coalitions based on that support. They will gain the opportunity to build support for the party platform; the party they represent, and the support they build, will result in acquiring a certain degree of political leverage.

Again, looking at the 1992 presidential election, Clinton got 43 percent of the popular vote and 370 electoral votes, G. H. W. Bush got 37.5 percent of the popular vote and 168 electoral votes, and Perot got 19 percent of the popular vote and zero electoral votes. As noted, it is not clear who would have won if Perot had not been in the race, as this change in the voting options would have changed the whole campaign process. Using approval voting, many voters may well have voted for two candidates—it is impossible to say who would have been the winner, or what the size of each candidate's support would have been. What we do know is that with approval voting and proportional distribution of electoral votes, the winner would have represented the result of an honest measure of voter support, with voters who honestly voted their concerns without having to waste their votes.

Approval voting and proportional distribution of electoral votes would assure that the voter's choice decides the outcome of the election—the outcome would not be distorted as a result of the corporate protectors' rules, which currently control the process. Winner take all, the rule in most states, greatly enhances the power of the corporate protectors to control the conversation and to influence the outcome of general presidential elections. The election conversation takes place in a few states, thus allowing for the focusing of most corporate spending in those states; most of that spending is on negative, sixty-second ads. These negative ads put candidates on the defensive and cause them to spend campaign time and money on distracting sham issues; this means that they have virtually no time to clarify the major challenges and opportunities that the nation faces. Hence, campaign time does not get spent on carefully describing programs that would address the people's interests (and might also threaten corporate interests). The corporate media helps the corporate protectors by focusing almost all of their attention on the race, and not on any in-depth discussion of issues in the swing states that decide the outcome of elections.

Section 9: Delegate Assignments

Following a presidential primary in which a political party uses approval voting, each candidate in the race will be assigned delegates to his/her party's national convention in proportion to his/her voter support.

Reasons for Section 9

The Democratic and Republican political party bosses use three methods for assigning delegates in the primaries. Each allows them to maximize the power of money in order to influence the outcome of the election and to minimize the likelihood of any political discussions that would adversely affect corporate interests. The three methods are: first, rules that require a threshold level of support before a candidate is assigned delegates; this system results in a significantly compressed field of viable candidates after the first few primaries. Second, the so-called proportional allocation of delegates in many states, which fails to meet any test of proportionality. And third, the existence of "super-delegate" votes, which can be cast by the delegate without any correlation to voter support.

The rules for running the primaries are designed to maximize the importance of the early primaries in narrowing the field of candidates as quickly as possible. Narrowing the field minimizes the number of voters who will have a meaningful say in the selection of candidates, and it maximizes the chances for the corporate-interest protectors to influence the choice of the political party's nominees. Narrowing the field of candidates also reduces the chances and likelihood that any candidate will discuss in a meaningful way and issues that might conflict with the corporate agenda.

The political parties' rules for assigning delegates are a key factor in narrowing the field of candidates. The field usually narrows from eight to twelve candidates to two or three viable candidates after the first two contests (in Iowa and New Hampshire), and it narrows further to two candidates—or sometimes only one—after the first five state contests. The original field of eight to twelve candidates generally gets whittled down to two or three candidates who are likely to gain more than 15 percent of the vote in the first two primaries. The two in front will usually have a total of about 45 percent, with the other eight splitting the remaining 55 percent of the vote. The two frontrunners do not necessarily have the broadest support of the voters; they could be fringe candidates who have strong 20 to 30 percent support, and not much support beyond that, and their support may not be split very much with other candidates. Only the candidates who have more than 15 percent of the votes, however (or at times 20 percent) will be allocated delegates. The result of this system is that they are declared the winners by the main news media—declared to be the top-tier candidates. Hence the voters in the later primaries get the message that you can either choose between these front runners or you can waste your vote.

Often, over half the media coverage of primary races takes place before and during the first two primaries of the Republican and Democratic parties. As a result, the first two primaries, in Iowa and New Hampshire—small states whose residents' concerns are not representative of most of the rest of the country—decide the fate of most of the candidates.

Under the present rules, the number of delegates who are assigned to a candidate is not closely correlated with his or her voter support. In addition, with the collapsing of the field of candidates, the delegates who were allocated to a certain candidate as a result of voter support may well decide to choose to support a different candidate instead. One should note that this change represents a change in delegate support, and not a change in voter support. The 2004 Democratic primary race had the following results:

Table 1. 2004 Democratic primary results

	Kerry	**Edwards**	**Dean**	**Kucinich**	**Clark**
Vote count (1,000)	9,871	3,133	894	617	536
Delegate count	2,573	559	167	40	60

Kucinich, in the 2004 race, was consistent in making comments that were critical of the corporate agenda. Kucinich's vote count was 69 percent of Dean's vote count, but his delegate count was 23 percent of Dean's delegate count. Furthermore, Kucinich's vote was 15 percent higher than Clark's vote count, but Kucinich's delegate count was 33 percent lower than Clark's delegate count.

In the 2004 Democratic primary, Kerry became the top-tier candidate after only the first five primaries. Kerry's speech to a Senate committee as a decorated naval officer upon his return from Vietnam (in which he advocated an end to that war) was very helpful to him in the early primaries. He soon made it clear, however, that he was not going to offend the corporate protectors by advocating a quick end to the war in Iraq; instead, he was going to fight the war more effectively—he was going to add forty-three thousand more troops to active duty. It became clear that to vote for a candidate in the 2004 presidential primary race who called for ending the war in Iraq—in this case, Kucinich—was to knowingly waste your vote, even though a majority of the voters wanted an end to that conflict.

The second method of control is the so-called proportionality rules. The following is typical of the lack of proportionality in the delegate count at the political party's national nominating convention. The 1988 Democratic primary race showed the following results.

Table 2: 1988 Democratic primary race results

	Dukakis	Jackson	Gore
Vote count	9,898,000	6,789,000	3,185,000
Delegate count	2,877	1,219	0

Note that the total of Jackson's and Gore's vote count is greater than Dukakis's vote count, but the total of their delegates is less than half of Dukakis's delegate count.

In the 2008 Democratic primary race, in which Hillary Clinton and Barack Obama were the main contenders, the corporate protectors were not able to reduce the field of candidates to one candidate early in the race. The result was that the competitors actually talked (guardedly) about a few issues that people wanted to hear about at least some of the time. The longer primary race resulted in greater voter turnout: 37,169,000 voters voted in the 2008 Democratic primary race. In comparison, since most votes in the 2004 Democratic primary were meaningless, and the election conversation did not threaten the corporate agenda, only 16,181,000 people bothered to vote. The total vote in 2004 was less than either the vote for Obama or for Clinton in 2008. It appears that voters become interested in the election if the candidates speak to their concerns, even if they do so guardedly.

The third method of control is the phenomenon of super-delegates. A significant number of delegates are allowed to vote for their choice of candidate as a result of their importance in one of the main political parties. The fact that they have a vote as a delegate has nothing to do with any one candidate's voter support, and they are not committed to any one candidate.

In the 2008 Democratic primary race, Hillary Clinton won the vote count, but lost the delegate count and the nomination. The difference was the super-delegate vote, as we may see from Tables 3 and 4.

Table 3: 2008 Democratic primary race results

	Obama	**Clinton**
Vote count	17,584,692	17,857,501
Delegate count	2,265.5	1,953

Table 4: Delegates before adding super-delegates

	Obama	**Clinton**
Delegate count	1828.5	1726
Super-delegate count	478	276.5

If we switch the allocation of super-delegates so that Obama receives Clinton's super-delegates and Clinton receives Obama's super-delegates, then Clinton wins. This example shows that the political party operatives can decide the outcome of the presidential nominating process, and not the voters. Note also that Obama's delegate count before adding the super-delegates was greater than Clinton's, even though her vote count was greater.

In an ideal world, in the presidential primaries, the candidates could run for office based on their ability to articulate plans and programs that would address the challenges and opportunities that face the nation, and based on their ability to convince the voters that they can and will work effectively if elected. And in a healthy democracy, the voters should have the opportunity to hear an effective vetting of the candidates and to express themselves with their vote, and to have their vote have some level of equivalency with other votes in the choice of the presidential candidate for their political party.

Unfortunately for the health of our democracy, the reality deviates drastically from the ideal. It is extremely difficult for a candidate to run for the presidency and to do well in the early primaries without having very significant financial backing. It is often sufficient for a candidate to have huge financial backing going into the early primaries in order to be considered a top-tier candidate; this consideration is based on that financial backing and vague "feel-good" statements of intent about their performance in office.

The combination of approval voting and proportional allocation of delegates would assure that each candidate would receive an honest level of voter support that is not distorted by having his or her support split with other candidates who have similar appeal, and the candidate's delegate allocation will be an honest reflection of his or her voter support. This would mean that fringe candidates could not be declared the winner—a top-tier candidate—based on 20 or 30 percent voter support that was the result of split votes among the other candidates. This honest measure of support for each candidate and the honest allocation of delegates would mean that candidates who have broad appeal—but similar appeal as other candidates—would survive the early primaries. This would decrease the importance of the early primaries, which would allow for significant increases in the number of voters who have a meaningful say in the selection of the presidential nominee. Decreasing the importance of the early primaries would also result in more voters being better informed, because the race would not be terminated before it had really begun. Most voters would become more interested in following the discussions, since they would know that their voting was more than a mere patriotic act—it would be part of the decision-making process. The health of our democracy requires that voters, not money, have the say in determining nominees for president.

Section 10: The Redistricting of Congressional Districts

The president, with the approval of the Senate, shall appoint a Redistricting Commission with staggered, fifteen-year terms for commission members. The commission will determine the broad principles (in consonance with the US Constitution) that will guide the redistricting of congressional districts after each new census, and will then supervise the process of redistricting so that the process remains consistent with the principles that have been set forth.

Reasons for Section 10

The opportunity to redraw the congressional map is another opportunity for the political party operatives in the majority party at the state level to enhance their political power.

In January of 2013, Joe Scarborough, US Republican congressman, stated, as reported by the *Huffington Post*:

> But I just have to say one other really important point…we actually got a minority of votes nationwide in [the] House races. It was just gerrymandering from 2010 that gave us the majority.

(The tally was two hundred thirty-three Republicans to two hundred Democrats.). The party which controls the state legislature is often able to manipulate the congressional district map and thus enhance the politicians' opportunities to protect vested interests at the expense of the people's interests, maintain their incumbency without accountability, and suppress meaningful political conversations. Thus the political party bosses of the party in power are able to extend their control in the state without any increase in popular approval—and even in some cases with a decrease in voter approval.

Computer-generated records make state voting records throughout the state readily available, and constructing proposed congressional district maps that are favorable to a particular political party easy to do. In 2010, the Tea Party wing of the Republican Party gained control of the state governments of several states. Many state governments aggressively used the chance to redraw the congressional district map to gain political advantage. This is not a new trick—both of the political parties have used it in the past, but never so aggressively or so effectively, and the courts have never in the past been so cooperative in allowing political officials to act in ways that enhance their political power. The courts seem to be especially cooperative when that enhancement can (and likely will) be used to further the corporate interests.

In 2010, in the eighteen Congressional races in Pennsylvania, sixty-seven thousand more votes were cast for Democratic congressional candidates than for Republican congressional candidates, but the Republicans won thirteen of the races and the Democrats only five. Similar disproportionate results happened in Ohio, Michigan, and Wisconsin.

In addition to packing a disproportionate amount of strength into a few districts, the map can be constructed so that two strong incumbents of the opposition party can be put in the same district so that they have to run against each other, and one will lose in the primary race. Particularly strong candidates of the opposition party are sometimes targeted by redrawing their districts so that they will have a difficult time winning—this was done to Dennis Kucinich in the 2012 congressional race.

The national population census is done every ten years, which necessitates redistricting as a result of uneven population gains and losses in the states. These map games that the political party bosses who are in control at the state level play when they engage in redistricting corrupt our democracy; prevent the popular will from being expressed; devalue certain votes, while increasing the value of other votes; and undermine democracy by restricting the political conversation. Many goals that need to be achieved when redistricting are necessary, but they should be decided at the national level: at the level where principles are established to guide the process. The maps should not be drawn at the state level, where they are not guided by principles, but rather are guided by the goal of gaining political advantage for the political party bosses who control that state. Our congressional representatives make national laws, not state laws; the laws they make have national consequences.

The congressional races are compressed to the primaries, instead of the general election, of either the Democratic or Republican Party as a result of carefully drawn congressional district maps. This compression of the congressional races restricts the field of candidates who will have a reasonable chance of winning to candidates who are members of either the Democratic or Republican Party, robs most voters of a say in the outcome of the election, increases the power of money spent to determine the outcome of the election by significantly reducing the field of possible candidates, and focuses the loyalty of the elected representative on the political party that elected him or her, rather than on all of the people of the district he or she represents and the nation at large. Reducing the field of candidates, and reducing the number of voters to the loyal members of the main political parties—those who vote in the political party primaries—allows the focus of corporate money that is spent to be spent on a much smaller group of candidates, and on a much smaller group of voters who have a say in the outcome of the election.

Deciding congressional races in the primaries stifles the political conversation of national issues at the state level, robs most voters of the opportunity to be informed about national issues, prevents voters from being meaningfully and intellectually involved with national issues, and robs them of a representative who will respond to their concerns about national issues. This also results in a narrow, partisan, political conversation in Congress, which has had very low public approval for the last several years as a result of its extremely partisan performance in office.

In addition, the compression of the race to the political party primaries reduces the voters' ability to hold the representatives accountable for their performance in Congress: representatives in politically lopsided districts are returned to office without any real discussion of their performance in office. The political party renominates its representative,

since he or she is a winning candidate for the majority political party in that district—and so winning becomes the issue.
The Congressional campaign becomes a narrow partisan
conversation, followed by partisan political posturing in
Congress.

The guiding principles for redistricting should be decided
by a proposed Federal Redistricting Commission. The maps
should be drawn by computer programs that are designed to
consider the priorities of the commission, and the maps should
be consistent with those priorities. This would be a major step
in making our congressional representatives accountable to the
people.

Section 11: Independent and Diverse Media

(11a) The Federal Communications Commission (FCC) and
the aforementioned proposed Public Media Board will cooperate to direct the divestiture of mainstream media corporations
from other corporations.

(11b) The FCC and the PMB will cooperate to ensure diversity of ownership of mainstream news media corporations.

Reasons for Section 11(a)
As President Thomas Jefferson wrote to Judge John Tyler in
1804:

> No experiment can be more interesting than that we are
> now trying, and which we trust will end in establishing
> the fact, that man may be governed by reason and truth.

Our first object should therefore be, to leave open to him all the avenues to truth. The most effectual hitherto found, is the freedom of the press. It is, therefore, the first shut up by those who fear the investigation of their actions.

Interesting words: "Our first object should be...to leave open to him all the avenues to truth," and not just the truths that are arrived at by asking, "How does this information affect the corporate interests?" The health of our democracy depends on the appropriate functioning of the mainstream news media.

The majority of voters acquire their information about the performance of the government and about candidates for federal office from mainstream news media. Mainstream news media are critical components in the corporate-interest protectors' control of the aforementioned "sound system" for the federal election process. The ownership and control of the mainstream news media by large corporations—often international corporations with broad commercial interests that are profoundly affected by government policies—close most avenues to truth for the majority of voters.

For more than a hundred years, federal and state laws have sought to restrict the corrupting influence of corporate monies on federal elections, on the formulation of federal policies, and on the accountability (or lack thereof) of elected officials to their performance in office. The laws and the Supreme Court, however, have recognized that an exception has to be made for laws that restrict media corporations' and the mainstream news media's First Amendment rights: the rights to free speech and freedom of the press.

As Thurgood Marshall said in the Supreme Court's opinion of *Austin v. Michigan Chamber of Commerce* (1990):

> [Media corporations differ in that] their resources are devoted to the collection of information and its dissemination to the public… [Restrictions on expenditures, therefore] might discourage news broadcasters or publishers from serving their crucial societal role.

This news media exception that Justice Marshall spoke of allows some international corporations to play a substantial role in federal elections and the formulation of governmental policies: the type of influential role that other laws seek to prevent. The ownership of the mainstream news media provides these media corporations with opportunities to influence government policy, and to assist other corporate-interest protectors in controlling the election sound system. The top management of corporate media companies are on the boards—and are paid very well for being on these boards—of other major corporations. These corporate protectors golf, hunt, and vacation together; keep second homes in the same locations; and have children who often marry other "royalty" and then join the team to further the corporate agenda that protects their financial interests.

The large media corporations have an implied agreement with the government: you do what you can to allow us freedom to run our corporations to the greatest financial advantage (even when that advantage conflicts with the people's interests), and we will strive to run a news program that will not hold the government accountable for policies, programs, and performance in office, especially when the governmental actions support and further the corporate agenda.

The goal of this part of the VRA is to free the mainstream news media from the corrupting influence of serving the corporate interests, and of serving government officials' interests that are not supportive of a healthy democracy. In 1911, the government ordered the breakup of Standard Oil because the firm's size and monopolistic practices were detrimental to the general welfare. In 1982, the government ordered the breakup of the Bell System, as it was determined that the company's control of the communications system was detrimental to the general welfare. Likewise, it is essential to separate the mainstream news media from the control of large corporations if we want to protect the democratic process. The coverage of the national news cannot be that small part of the corporate plan that is designed, shaped, and delivered to further broaden corporate goals—which are often determined by the CEO of the corporation.

Reasons for Section 11 (b)
In 1983, fifty corporations controlled 90 percent of the media market. In contrast, in 2011, only six corporations controlled 90 percent of the media market. Arguably the most powerful person in the presidential electoral process is Rupert

Murdoch, CEO and the controlling voice of News Corp, one of the six largest media corporations. News Corp owns *Fox News*, the *Wall Street Journal*, and other media outlets. Political analysts claim that Murdoch can influence millions of voters. His influence does not originate from his ability to have his ideas compete in the marketplace of ideas; rather, his influence comes from his control of the conversation in a very significant segment of the place where ideas are marketed. In this place, ideas do not compete: they are consistently and repeatedly proclaimed as truths. The mainstream media protectors of the corporate agenda proclaim their allegiance to free-market principles, but they consistently support monopolistic control. They work toward monopolistic control in the area of mainstream media.

Mitt Romney, in his 2012 presidential race, met with the editorial writers of the *Wall Street Journal*, with Murdoch attending, on at least two occasions to seek the paper's support. In 2015, Murdoch made it clear that he would not support another Romney candidacy—and Romney withdrew his name as a possible candidate.

The prime ministers of Great Britain had a very close relationship with Murdoch for more than two decades. Those relationships have been derailed in that country, since the journalists for his newspapers in Britain have been found guilty of illegal wiretaps, bribery of police officers, and interfering in a murder investigation. News Corp has paid over $400 million to settle claims that have resulted from the wiretaps. During the trial of News Corp in May 2012, Murdoch was reported to have stated, "I give instructions to my editors all round the world, why shouldn't I in London?" One has to wonder if "the United States" could easily be substituted for "London" in this statement. A report from the British Parliament states that "Rupert Murdoch is not a fit person to exercise the stewardship of a major international company." The appropriateness of his controlling a large US media corporation has not been questioned by our Congress: no investigations, and no reports.

In 1983, the FCC did not allow any corporation to own more than forty radio stations, but by 1995 Clear Channel owned twelve hundred radio stations. In 2007, the shareholders approved a buyout, thus allowing Clear Channel to proceed with becoming a private entity and ending thirty-five years as a public company. In 2008, Bain Capital, the private-equity firm started and managed by Romney, bought Clear Channel. Premiere Radio Networks is one of the subsidiaries of Clear Channel, which syndicates ninety radio programs and reaches over 150 million listeners weekly. Rush Limbaugh, Glen Beck, Sean Hannity, and several other big-name news talk-show hosts are on the Premiere Radio Network team. Presidential candidates should not be allowed to have such influence over the owners of the mainstream news media outlet that has the largest audience in the country. This section of the amendment would require divestiture of ownership in order to end the control of large segments of the news media by single or small groups of individuals.

Section 12: Protecting the Franchise

(12a) All states will facilitate the right to vote by ensuring minimal disruption in the verification of voter identity.

(12b) All states are required to provide convenient early voting in federal elections.

(12c) Felons who have completed their sentences will be allowed to vote.

Reasons for Section 12(a)

Our history is full of stories of schemes by the group in political power (both at the national and state level) trying to restrict the vote to the citizens who can be relied on to support their agenda and to keep them in power. At the time the Constitution was written, slaves and free blacks were counted as three-fifths of a person for the purpose of taking the census. At that time, only white males were eligible to vote—blacks and women enhanced the value of white males' vote by increasing the number of electoral votes in a state: and thus the number of US representatives. This was especially significant in the Southern states: the numbers of blacks and women increased the political power of the state without diluting the political potency of the voting group. The three-fifths rule was decisive in electing several Southerners presidents before the onset of the Civil War.

The right to vote is compromised by directly suppressing the vote, indirectly suppressing the vote, reducing the meaningfulness of votes, and distorting the relative value of votes. The corporate protectors use all of these methods to control the electoral process. These methods complement one another, and, in combination, they are very effective in controlling the electoral process.

This section of the proposed amendment focuses on direct suppression of the vote. The other sections of the amendment address the other methods of corrupting the electoral process.

Under the Constitution, written in 1787, neither women nor blacks had the right to vote. Extending the right to vote to blacks was resisted most strongly by those who felt it would threaten their power base. In 1870, five years after the end of the Civil War, the Fifteenth Amendment to the Constitution was ratified to ensure that the newly freed slaves had the right to vote:

> *Section 1.* The right of citizens of the United States to vote shall not be denied or abridged by the United States or by any state on account of race, color, or previous condition of servitude.
>
> *Section 2.* The Congress shall have power to enforce this article by appropriate legislation.

In 1920, after more than seventy years of organized struggle, women gained the right to vote with the passage of the Nineteenth Amendment, which stated:

> The right of citizens of the United States to vote shall not be denied or abridged by the United States or by any State on account of sex.

Some influential upper-class women opposed the amendment, fearing that it would dilute their influence. The Democratic and Republican Party bosses were able to ignore the Fifteenth Amendment and to successfully suppress the vote for nearly a century. States enacted poll taxes, taxes that individuals were to pay if they were to have the right to vote. In many states this was done to make it very difficult for blacks and poor whites to vote. Literacy tests, often administered unfairly, were also introduced in some states as a way to deny people the right to vote. Until the Civil Rights movement of the 1950s and 1960s, which resulted in the passage of the Voting Rights Act in 1965, physical intimidation and financial intimidation—from loss of job opportunities to outright violence—were often used to suppress the vote.

The strength and depth of the intimidation is captured by the following quote from an interview with John Lewis, thirteen-term US Representative from Georgia, on *Democracy Now!* on December 24, 2012:

> On March 7, 1965, a group of us attempted to march from Selma to Montgomery, Alabama, to dramatize to the nation that people wanted to register to vote…And we got to the top of the bridge. We saw a sea of blue—Alabama state troopers—and we continued to walk. We came within hearing distance of the state troopers. And a man identified himself and said, "I'm Major John Cloud of the Alabama State Troopers. This is an unlawful march. It will not be allowed to continue. I give you three minutes to disperse and return to your

church." And one of the young people walking with me, leading the march, a man by the name of Hosea Williams, who was on the staff of Dr. Martin Luther King Jr., said, "Major, give us a moment to kneel and pray." And the major said, "Troopers, advance!" And you saw these guys putting on their gas masks. They came toward us, beating us with nightsticks and bullwhips, trampling us with horses.

I was hit in the head by a state trooper with a nightstick. I had a concussion at the bridge. My legs went out from under me. I felt like I was going to die. I thought I saw Death.

It is unreal, it is unbelievable, and that at this time in our history, forty-seven years after the Voting Rights Act was passed and signed into law that we're trying to go backward. I think there is a systematic, deliberate attempt on the part of so many of these states…to keep people from participating.

The Voting Rights Act of 1965 passed the Senate 77 to 19, and the House 333 to 85. It included several key remedial provisions, particularly Section 5, that were slated to expire unless renewed. These provisions have been renewed several times. They were most recently renewed in 2006, for twenty-five years. After a debate and discussion, the provisions passed the Senate 98 to 0, and the House 390 to 33.

In June 2013, the five Supreme Court corporate protectors gutted the Voting Rights Act in *Shelby County v. Holder.* This ruling is inconsistent with Section 2 of the Fifteenth

Amendment, that "Congress shall have power to enforce this article [the power to protect the right to vote] by appropriate legislation." Justice Scalia, commenting on the vote to renew the Voting Rights Act, during oral argument stated:

> I am fairly confident it will be reenacted in perpetuity unless—unless a court can say it does not comport with the Constitution...It's—it's a concern that this is not the kind of a question you can leave to Congress.

Again, Section 2 of the Fifteenth Amendment states that "Congress shall have power to enforce this article by appropriate legislation." Justice Ginsberg wrote a dissent, joined by Justices Breyer, Sotomayor, and Kagan:

> "Voting discrimination still exists; no one doubts that." (Quoting the majority opinion.) But the Court today terminates the remedy that proved to be best suited to block that discrimination. The Voting Rights Act of 1965 has worked to combat voting discrimination where other remedies had been tried and failed.

Justice Scalia also stated in oral argument:

> I think it is attributable, very likely attributable, to a phenomenon that is called perpetuation of racial entitlement...that lawmakers had only voted to renew the act in 2006 because there wasn't anything to be gained politically from voting against it.

Justice Sotomayor responded, questioning the thinking that the right to vote is a *racial entitlement*. Justice Ginsberg further wrote in dissent:

> It cannot tenably be maintained that the [Voting Rights Act], an Act of Congress adopted to shield the right to vote from racial discrimination, is inconsistent with the letter or spirit of the Fifteenth Amendment, or any provision of the Constitution read in light of the Civil War Amendments.

The five Supreme Court corporate-interest protectors make it difficult (if not impossible) to hold our elected representatives in Congress accountable for allowing direct suppression of the vote, particularly those votes that are likely to be opposed to the corporate agenda. This decision puts a signal out that the Supreme Court will provide room for the states to control the franchise. Many states took advantage of the opportunity that the Supreme Court gave them to control the franchise: to pass laws that allegedly protect against voter fraud, which, as mentioned earlier, has not been a verifiable problem for several decades. These voter fraud protection laws are indeed a voter fraud, in that they suppress legitimate voters' right to vote.

Passing unfair voter identification laws represents one method for suppressing the vote. In 2011, Texas passed one of the most restrictive voter ID laws, called Bill 14. This bill was at first blocked under Section 5 of the Voting Rights Act, but after the Supreme Court effectively struck down that section in *Shelby v. Holder* in 2013, Texas officials announced that they would start enforcing the ID law.

Bill 14 was challenged a second time. A federal district court, after a two-week trial, determined that Bill 14 would have a prohibited discriminatory effect on minority voters, and would prevent more than six hundred thousand registered voters from voting for lack of compliant identification. The district court determined that Bill 14 operated as an unconstitutional tax that abridged citizens' right to vote. The lead witness in the district court trial was an elderly woman named Sammie Louise Bates, who testified via video. Bates grew up in Mississippi in the 1940s, and remembered smoldering with rage as she counted out money so that her grandmother could pay the state's notorious poll tax. Bates has voted regularly since she was twenty-one. Today, she lives on social security and little else. After trying (unsuccessfully) to cast a ballot that would count in 2013, she learned that she would have to pay forty-two dollars to procure birth records from Mississippi if she wanted to vote again. Sitting at a burnished conference table in a law firm's office, Bates was quizzed about why she had not quickly procured the paperwork. "I had to put forty-two dollars where it was doing the most good. It was feeding my family," she explained. She gazed evenly at her questioner: "We couldn't eat the birth certificate."

The federal district court stated that Bill 14 was irreconcilable even with the Supreme Court's gutted Voting Rights Act of 1965, because the former determined that it was enacted with a racially discriminatory purpose. Bill 14 was allegedly passed to prevent voter fraud from citizens voting illegally. The district court found that Texas did not begin to demonstrate that the bill's discriminatory features were necessary to prevent illegal voting. The court observed that "The Texas Legislature and Governor had an evident incentive to 'gain partisan advantage by suppressing votes of African-Americans and Latinos.'" The district court placed an injunction on the enforcement of Bill 14.

A federal appeals court then placed a stay on the injunction, contending that preventing the enforcement of Bill 14 would be disruptive to the voting process. The case was appealed to the US Supreme Court, which did not take up the case and allowed Bill 14 to take effect without comment.

Justice Ginsburg dissented from this ruling, joined by justices Sotomayor and Kagan. (This was an unusual case: there was a written dissent to a Supreme Court ruling, but not a written opinion.) In her dissent, Justice Ginsberg summarized the strong case that the district court had for prohibiting Bill 14 from taking effect. She concluded her dissent with the following:

> The greatest threat to public confidence in elections in this case is the prospect of enforcing a purposefully discriminatory law, one that likely imposes an unconstitutional poll tax and risks denying the right to vote to hundreds of thousands of eligible voters.

Texas had done very little to inform the public about the new, required procedures for voting, or to provide sufficient information about the procedures that were necessary for acquiring one's voter ID. Only 340 voters of the estimated six hundred thousand registered voters who were potentially denied the right to vote by this law managed to obtain their state voter ID.

Several other states have passed voter ID laws that suppress the vote. Pennsylvania, for example, passed a voter ID law. When the supporters of the Pennsylvania law—some of whom had alleged that the law was passed to prevent voter fraud—were asked in court, "What evidence do you have of voter fraud as a result of illegal voting?" they had to reply that they had none. The Pennsylvania Supreme Court did not allow the law to be enforced. Georgia, Indiana, and Florida also have strict voter ID laws.

Purging the registered voting list without good reason to do so is another method that is used to suppress the vote. The *New York Times* reported that tens of thousands of voters may have been illegally purged from the rolls in swing states. In Montana, US District Court Judge Donald Molloy denounced the state Republican Party's efforts to challenge the registration of six thousand voters, writing: "The timing of the challenges is so transparent it defies common sense to believe the purpose is anything but political chicanery." In Florida, any registered voter (or poll watcher) of a county can challenge the right of anyone from that county to vote. Florida has a "Voter Registration Verification Law," better known as the "No Match, No Vote" standard: the voter registration has to match another database in order to verify the legitimacy of the registration. Twenty-seven states now participate in the Interstate Voter Registration Crosscheck Program, which provides the same kinds of opportunities to deny the vote as the illegal literacy tests.

Justice Ginsberg, in June 2013, wrote in her dissenting opinion of the gutting of the Voting Rights Act that "this Court repeatedly encountered the remarkable 'variety and persistence' of laws disenfranchising minority citizens." She further stated that the Voting Rights Act had been the most effective means to combat these efforts. These five corporate Supreme Court justices need further guidance on the legitimacy of laws that are designed to protect the right to vote.

Reasons for Section 12(b)

Election day is traditionally on a Tuesday, a work day. At one time, some states made election day a holiday or required employers to give workers time off to vote. This is no longer true, although government workers often have a holiday. Quite often, long lines and long waiting times await those who want to vote. This is particularly true in those polling areas where the majority of voters support the presidential candidate of the political party that is not in control of the state government. In the most recent presidential elections, people were reported to have had to wait more than ten hours to vote. Long waits serve to discourage the working class but are less onerous on the wealthy who can choose the time they want to go to the polls. Another ploy is to make it confusing about where one is supposed to vote. Again, this almost universally happens in voting locations where the voters do not support the political party in power in the state. In a healthy democracy, every effort should be made to increase, rather than suppress, voter turnout.

Reasons for Section 12(c)

The United States has more citizens in prison per capita than any other nation, and a grossly disproportionate number of the prison population are minorities and/or poor. While studies have shown that the proportion of whites and blacks that are (or have been) involved in the use of illegal drugs is approximately the same, the proportion of blacks that have been convicted of drug crimes is much higher. Black Americans are more than three times as likely to be arrested for marijuana possession as white Americans.

There has been a great deal of academic discussion about the crimes committed on Wall Street that contributed in a meaningful way to the economic crash of 2008, but nobody involved in the Wall Street debacle has been charged with a crime. The Obama administration has prosecuted several whistle-blowers and have found them guilty, but the individuals whom the whistleblowers exposed—who committed serious crimes—were fined, but not charged. In many states, the whistle-blower loses his or her right to vote. Furthermore, some felony charges have to do with personal weaknesses (such as addiction), and do not reflect in any way the individual's concern for the public good, or for the person's ability to discern what the public good might be.

What is the downside of allowing people who have been convicted of a felony to vote? People vote out of a sense of civic duty, knowing that their votes will have little or no chance of making a difference, and that they have virtually no chance of personal gain in exercising that privilege. Instead, their only hope is that their vote might make a difference if they are voting as members of a group that strives to initiate peaceful governmental change by appropriate citizen involvement. Appropriate collective political involvement is what the corporate-interest protectors want to minimize, but it is what the health of our democracy depends upon.

Section 13: The Appointment of Supreme Court Justices

(13a) A person nominated by the president to be a justice of the Supreme Court shall answer truthfully and fully all senators' questions about issues that may come before the Supreme Court. All information pertinent to the confirmation will be made available to the Senate. The president shall nominate candidates based on their public records and not on secret interviews. The minimum age of a candidate shall be sixty.

(13b) The Public Media Board will select several independent groups to lead discussions on public media (and on government-purchased time on other media) about the confirmation hearing and the arguments for and against confirmation. The PMB will have access to all information that is made available to the Senate.

Reasons for Section 13(a)

The appointment process for Supreme Court justices consists of the president nominating a candidate, the Senate Judiciary Committee holding hearings, and then the whole Senate briefly discussing the appropriateness of the nominee and voting to confirm or reject the nomination. The senators universally agree that the vote to confirm a nominee as one of nine justices on the Supreme Court is one of their most serious decisions. The following statements point to the importance of the confirmation process. The quotations are from the confirmation process of John Roberts for Chief Justice of the Supreme Court. Similar introductory comments have been made for the confirmation of other Supreme Court justices for at least last thirty years.

> SENATOR LEAHY: Ours is a government of laws. When we are faced with a vacancy on the Supreme Court, we're reminded that it's our fellow citizens, nine out of our 280 million Americans, who interpret and apply those laws. Chief among emerging concerns are whether the Supreme Court will continue its recent effort to restrict the authority of Congress to pass legislation to protect the people's interests.
>
> SENATOR KENNEDY: Today, grandparents who were denied the right to vote expect their grandsons and granddaughters to be able to cast a ballot without discrimination or intimidation. We expect our

courts to defend our progress as their constitutional responsibility.

SENATOR BIDEN: The people of the United States are entitled to know as much as they can about the person we are entrusting with and safeguarding our future, and the future of our children and our grandchildren.

SENATOR FEINSTEIN: If you, Judge Roberts, subscribe to the Rehnquist Court's restrictive interpretation of Congress's ability to legislate, the impact could be enormous...the Rehnquist Court has weakened or invalidated more than three dozen federal statutes. Almost a third of these decisions were based on the commerce clause and the Fourteenth Amendment.

The Senate Judiciary Committee holds several days of televised hearings and then votes to recommend to the whole Senate either to confirm or to reject the confirmation. Many senators on the Judiciary Committee spoke extensively about the need for Judge Roberts to answer questions candidly, avoiding vague generalities. For example, Senator Feingold stated:

It is the Senate Judiciary Committee's job to ask tough questions. We are tasked by the Senate with getting a complete picture of your qualifications, your temperament and how you will carry out your duties.

Senator Feingold further quoted Senator Grassley from the confirmation hearings of Justice O'Connor:

> I do not agree that commenting on past Supreme Court decisions is a commitment to hold a certain way on future cases. And I feel that in order that we as senators fulfill our duty, it is incumbent on us to discover a nominee's judicial philosophy.

In the 1987 hearings for the confirmation of Robert Bork, a Reagan nominee, Judge Bork willingly answered questions. The senators heard concerns from their constituents and were required to vote, knowing that many voters had followed the hearings carefully and were concerned about how their senators would vote. This process resulted in forty-two senators voting for confirmation, and fifty-eight against. Ever since Bork's confirmation hearing, all nominees have refused to answer certain questions, and some nominees have even refused to answer any questions that might shine a light on their judicial philosophy.

Clarence Thomas was nominated to the Supreme Court by George H. W. Bush on July 1, 1991. His hearing was contentious as a result of Anita Hill's testimony that Thomas had sexually harassed her when he was her boss at the Equal Employment Opportunity Commission (EEOC); the hearing was also contentious as a result of his conservative views. The facts were contested, but it was appropriate that her testimony was allowed and the public had the opportunity to hear it. Again, many voters were extremely interested in the hearings. Justice Thomas was confirmed by a vote of fifty-two in favor to forty-eight opposed. George H. W. Bush lost the presidential race in 1992, and it is reasonably clear that the Thomas hearings did not help him during that election.

Women were concerned about (and responded to) what they perceived as abuse of Anita Hill during the hearings; five new women were elected to the Senate in 1992; prior to that, in all Senate elections, only four women had been elected to the Senate for a full term. This a positive indicator of the health of our democracy; holding the president accountable for his nominee to the Supreme Court, some women decided that they have a role to play in the senate and held the senators accountable for their confirmation vote by challenging their incumbency.

Real accountability could split political party support and, in some cases, it should do just that. Political party bosses want the confirmation process to solidify the support of the party base without splitting support within the party—this takes careful scripting of the hearings, and the cooperation of the corporate mainstream media.

In order to assure minimal voter disagreement, the president has often chosen candidates who lack a substantial paper trail. Sometimes presidents decide not to release information about the nominees' work in government as lawyers, for instance. The nominee often refuses to answer nonsupportive questions, using the excuse that he or she should not be expressing opinions on issues that could come before the court.

Removing the excuse for not answering senators' questions mentioned above would be a major first step toward creating an authentic vetting process. The implication of this excuse is that somehow it would be unethical for a nominee to discuss his or her judicial philosophy if that philosophy is pertinent to a case that might come before the court.

The Supreme Court, in its opinion in *Republican Party v. White* (2002), spoke to the right of judicial candidates to answer questions in the vetting process. Justice Scalia wrote:

> Minnesota's Constitution has provided for the selection of all state judges by popular election...Since 1974, judicial candidates have been subject to a legal restriction which states that a "candidate for a judicial office, including an incumbent judge," shall not "announce his or her views on disputed legal or political issues."
>
> ...A judge's lack of predisposition regarding the relevant legal issues in a case has never been thought a necessary component of equal justice, and with good reason—it is virtually impossible to find a judge who does not have preconceptions about the law—avoiding judicial preconceptions on legal issues is neither possible nor desirable, pretending otherwise by attempting to preserve the "appearance" of that type of impartiality can hardly be a compelling state interest.

Justice Scalia delivered the opinion of the court in this case, and was joined by Chief Justice Rehnquist, along with Justices

O'Connor, Kennedy, and Thomas. The majority found the restriction to be unconstitutional.

This opinion speaks to state elections of state Supreme Court justices, but the opinion would be equally applicable to the right of a US Supreme Court nominee to "announce his or her views on disputed legal or political issues" during confirmation hearings. The senators' and the people's right to know the philosophy of a nominee represents a compelling state interest. There needs to be a full and honest vetting of the president's nominee for a position that is arguably the most important position in the federal government, with the possible exception of the presidency.

Justice Scalia went further in the opinion:

> This complete separation of the judiciary from the enterprise of "representative government" might have some truth in those countries where judges neither make law themselves nor set aside the laws enacted by the legislature. It is not a true picture of the American system...[T]hey have the immense power to shape the States' constitutions as well.

Senators from both parties have voiced their concerns that the immense power of a bare majority on the Supreme Court has crippled Congress's power to address important national issues by declaring legislation unconstitutional. Senator Grassley, among others, spoke to this concern during the Roberts confirmation hearing:

If we confirm individuals who are bent on assigning to themselves the power to fix society's problems as they see fit, a bare majority of these nine unelected and unaccountable men and women will usurp the power of the people, hijacking democracy to serve their own political prejudices.

Hence, it is important that a nominee answer questions directly during the confirmation process, and not in vague generalities. In *Republican Party v. White*, Justice Scalia also noted that the power of a state to choose its judges through election does not include the lesser power to conduct elections under conditions of state-imposed voter ignorance. We are approximating "a condition of state-imposed voter ignorance" in the confirmation process of Supreme Court justices. Accountability to the voters requires that the voters have good information as to the fitness of the nominee for the Supreme Court; accountability requires that a nominee answer all pertinent questions in the confirmation hearings.

The sixty-year-old minimum age recommended in the proposed amendment allows time for a candidate to gather adequate experience and a paper trail that makes it possible to properly assess candidates, and allows for accountability to the people for the choice of a nominee. This age requirement does not unduly burden the opportunity for the confirmed justice to serve on the court—the median retirement age of the last ten justices who retired was eighty.

Reasons for Section 13(b)

The rationale for section 13(b) provides strong support for all sections of this amendment: the need to wrest control of all three branches of the federal government from the plutocracy and to reestablish the First Amendment right to a free press, and not a corporate, plutocracy-controlled press.

Possibly, the most politically dangerous act for a senator is to aggressively question the appropriateness of confirming a Supreme Court nominee who has the strong support of the corporate interest protectors. It is not only politically dangerous, it is an act that is not at all likely to be effective; the corporate media will cover the supportive efforts and ignore non-supportive information. The Supreme Court confirmation process has evolved so that accountability is only to the plutocracy-protecting their interests.

The vetting of Justice John Roberts to become Chief Justice in 2005 points to the need for the proposed Public Media Board to ensure public access to good information about the appropriateness of the nominee for justice of the Supreme Court. The discussion of this process is not intended to suggest that Roberts should not have been confirmed but to show that the media failed in its duty to adequately inform the public.

The following facts about Judge Roberts were covered carefully by the corporate media: Justice Roberts graduated from Harvard with honor in history, completing the degree in three years. He graduated from Harvard Law School with honors, and was managing editor of the *Harvard Law Review*. He served as a law clerk to Federal Appeals Court

Judge Henry Friendly and then as law clerk for Chief Justice Rehnquist. He was Special Assistant to the US Attorney General in 1981–1982, Associate Counsel to President Ronald Reagan from 1982 to 1986, and Deputy Solicitor General under President George H. W. Bush (1989-1993). On the basis of education and experience, Justice Roberts, as the American Bar Association would indicate, was well qualified. This "well qualified" has nothing to do with his judicial philosophy, which is crucial to his performance as a Supreme Court Justice; often senators and the news referred to him as well qualified" as if it were conclusive.

Many of the following facts about John Roberts- particularly those which were possibly harmful to his confirmation- were not covered carefully, if at all, by the corporate media: after joining the Reagan administration, Roberts urged the Attorney General not to back an investigation of alleged sexual discrimination in the athletics programs at the University of Richmond, and not to intervene on behalf of female inmates in a sexual discrimination case involving job training for prisoners. Roberts also wrote a memorandum criticizing the Supreme Court decision, *Griswold v. Connecticut* (1965), recognizing a constitutional right to privacy and striking down a state law prohibiting contraceptive drugs or devices to married persons. Roberts belittled "the so-called 'right to privacy,'" which he claimed to be "an amorphous right...not to be found in the Constitution." As Associate Counsel to President Reagan, Roberts argued in favor of rolling back federal civil rights protections and dismantling programs that were aimed at remedying past discrimination. These policies were part of a larger strategy to limit the meaningful vote, thus putting control of suffrage in the hands of the political party bosses at the state level and promoting committed voter support on social issues while avoiding any meaningful discussion of the people's economic interests.

As Kenneth Starr's chief deputy as Solicitor General, Roberts represented the federal government (promoting the Bush administration's agenda) before the Supreme Court. Whenever possible—as cases to argue would allow—the Starr-Roberts team argued to dismantle school desegregation, weaken the separation of church and state, weaken abortion rights (Roberts filed a brief urging the Supreme Court to put restrictions on the advice that family planning clinics could give to women who were considering abortions, and stated that *Roe v. Wade* was "wrongly decided"), opposing affirmative action, enhancing the president's national security powers, and restricting individual, class action, and environmental law suits—all issues consistent with the agenda of protecting corporate interests.

When questioned about these statements and memoranda during the confirmation hearings by Senator Kennedy who questioned the appropriateness of these statements as a judicial philosophy for a Supreme Court justice, Roberts stated that his statements were made by a lawyer who was representing a client; when Senator Graham, who was a known supporter of his nomination, asked a similar question in a supportive way, however, the answer was entirely different:

GRAHAM: During your time of working with Ronald Reagan, were you ever asked to take a legal position that you thought was unethical or not solid?
ROBERTS: No, Senator, I was not.

No meaningful follow-up questions were asked concerning significant evidence that his judicial philosophy did not deviate substantially from Judge Bork's. This lack of investigation by the senators and the corporate media avoided any possible accountability to the voters for any senator's vote to confirm. This is representative of the broad problem of corporate-interest protectors' control of the political conversation, which works to avoid accountability to the voters.

The judicial ideas that Roberts expressed as Associate Counsel to President Reagan in memoranda would be ideas that one might expect from a member of the Federalist Society. The Federalist Society was founded in 1982 by conservatives and Libertarians. Judge Bork was one of the founding members; Justice Scalia, then a law professor at the University of Chicago, helped organize a chapter of the Federalist Society. When Roberts was asked if he had been a member of that society, he stated that he could not recall ever having been a member. On July 25, 2005, the *Washington Post* reported that John Roberts was listed in the society's 1997–1998 leadership directories as serving on the Steering Committee of the Federalist Society. The corporate media did not cover this substantive lack of recall; the story never got traction. One might compare this lack of media coverage with the media's treatment of Brian Williams' nonsubstantive faulty recall.

This is typical of the corporate media, which will aggressively demonstrate concern for honesty when it has an impact on a person, but not when it has an impact on the corporate agenda.

In 2003, President Bush nominated Roberts to the Court of Federal Appeals for the District of Columbia, to which he was quickly confirmed. In December 2004, Judge Roberts was assigned to a three-judge panel to hear an appeal of the *Hamdan v. Rumsfeld* case. To understand some of the defects in the questioning of Judge Roberts and the media coverage of the hearings, it is necessary to understand the main issues in the Hamdan case and to appreciate the importance of this case.

In 2003, the Bush administration set up a system of tribunals to try accused war criminals with no clear procedural safeguards for the accused, no limitation to the time or manner of detention before trial, and no restriction against torture—if convicted, the defendant could be subject to the death penalty. The Bush administration anticipated that these tribunals would prosecute a stream of accused defendants.

In June 2004, the Supreme Court ruled that the regular detainees could go to federal court to challenge the tribunal procedures. *Hamdan v. Rumsfeld* became the test case to determine the validity of the system. Hamdan, a prisoner at Guantanamo, filed suit in the Federal District Court against Bush's Secretary of Defense Rumsfeld.

Lt. Cmdr. Charles Swift of the US Navy was appointed defense counsel for Salim Hamdan. Hamdan had served as a driver for Osama bin Laden in Afghanistan. Swift's appointment letter indicated that his access to his client was conditioned on his negotiating a guilty plea. Swift later stated, "We'd been told we would never talk to the press, we would never be seen. We would simply sit there, take it, and then it would be over. It was to be a one-way show."

In 2004 the District Court granted habeas relief and the government appealed. On July 15, 2005, the three-judge panel, which included Judge Roberts, rejected Hamdan's human rights claim. In a two-to-one decision (Judge Roberts one of the two), the panel ruled that prisoners could not claim protection under the Geneva Convention.

> SENATOR GRAHAM [a Republican senator who supported his nomination]: Do you believe that the Geneva Convention, as a body of law, that it has been good for America to be part of that convention?
> JUDGE ROBERTS: I do, yes. My understanding in general is it's an effort to bring civilized standards to conduct of war—an effort to bring some protection and regularity to prisoners of war in particular. And I think that's a very important international effort...I applaud the president, because, in fighting the war on terror, we need not become our enemy. Our strength as a nation is believing in the rule of law, even for the worst of those that we may encounter...

There was virtually no discussion in the confirmation hearings or by corporate media about what Judge Roberts had ruled to be "acceptable procedures" for trying Hamdan, and no questioning of how "our strength as a nation is believing in the rule of law" was jeopardized by Judge Roberts's ruling in *Hamdan v. Rumsfeld*—a ruling that declared that we will not follow the rule of law. Judge Roberts's ruling cannot be interpreted as an "an effort to bring civilized standards to conduct of war...an effort to bring some protection and regularity to prisoners of war in particular." This discrepancy between his words and his action was not examined by the senators, nor by the corporate media.

After Judge Roberts had been confirmed as Chief Justice in 2005 and upon appeal of the *Hamdan* case to the U.S. Supreme Court, the Supreme Court in 2006 overturned the ruling of the Court of Appeals.

(Chief Justice Roberts had to recuse himself from this case as he had already ruled on the case).

Nina Totenberg covered the case on NPR:

> In the jargon of the Supreme Court, we talk about "landmark cases." Some, of course, are more landmark than others. But by any yardstick, the June 2006 ruling in *Hamdan v. Rumsfeld* was one for the history books.
>
> ... The court's 5-3 decision is widely seen as the most important ruling on executive power in decades, or perhaps ever.

Justice Stevens wrote the opinion for the court:

> These simply are not the circumstances in which, by any stretch of the historical evidence or this Court's precedents, a military commission established by

Executive Order…[m]ay lawfully try a person and subject him to punishment…

The Court of Appeals thought, and the Government asserts, that Common Article 3 [of the Geneva Convention] does not apply to Hamdan…That reasoning is erroneous.

Common Article 3, then, is applicable here…[and] requires that Hamdan be tried by a "regularly constituted court affording all the judicial guarantees which are recognized as indispensable by civilized peoples."

The Supreme Court's *Hamdan v. Rumsfeld* opinion clarifies what the Court of Appeals had ruled as being an acceptable trial process for Hamdan and other prisoners, and also why the court found the process unacceptable. The opinion found substantial deviations from the laws of war and domestic laws, including that the defendant and the defendant's attorney may be forbidden to view evidence used against the defendant; the defendant's attorney may be forbidden to discuss certain evidence with the defendant; and evidence including hearsay, unsworn live testimony, and statements gathered through torture may be admitted as evidence. While the media and the Senate could not have known how the Supreme Court would rule in *Hamdan*, the American people were entitled to know how the nominee perceived the fairness of the process in this case as a vignette of his judicial philosophy.

The timeline of the nomination and confirmation of Judge Roberts as Chief Justice of the Supreme Court also raised questions which should have been explored and publicized more thoroughly.

On July 1, 2005, Justice Sandra Day O'Connor announced her retirement plans. In her letter to George W. Bush, she stated that her retirement from active service would take effect upon the confirmation of her successor. As noted above, on July 15, 2005, the three-judge panel upon which Judge Roberts served rejected Hamdan's human rights claim. On July 19, 2005, President Bush nominated John Roberts to be a justice on the Supreme Court, replacing Justice O'Connor. At the time of the nomination, no discussion took place about the possible impropriety of the nomination so soon after an important court victory for the Bush administration and its exertion of presidential power.

In response to a Senate questionnaire, Roberts revealed that he had been interviewed for a possible Supreme Court nomination by Attorney General Alberto Gonzales on April 1, 2005; this was six days before oral argument in *Hamdan v. Rumsfeld* and happened before Justice O'Conner had indicated that she was going to resign. He was questioned about this by Senator Feingold during the hearings. His answers to the senator's questions about this interview revealed that this interview had led to a secret, call-back interview on May 3, but still no opening on the Supreme Court. Roberts was interviewed by six high government officials, including Vice President Dick Cheney; Andrew H. Card Jr., the White House chief of staff; Karl Rove, Bush's chief political strategist; and Attorney General Gonzales. One would expect that six top officials would not show up to hear Judge Roberts answer questions only in vague generalities (as he did during the Senate confirmation hearings). Roberts was interviewed again on May 3 by Harriet Miers, the White House counsel, and again on May 23. There also were phone conversations with the president's staff.

> FEINGOLD: You never informed the defense counsel in [the *Hamdan* case] of these meetings. Did you?
> ROBERTS: I did not, no.
> FEINGOLD: Mr. Gonzales's advice to the president concerning the Geneva Conventions was an issue in the case. Isn't that right?
> ROBERTS: I don't want to discuss anything about what's at issue in the case. The case is still pending before the Supreme Court.

Roberts's reason for not answering the senator's questions about information that is part of the public record of the *Hamdan v. Rumsfeld* case was inappropriate. Not only was this material part of the public record, but if he were to be confirmed, he knew that he would have to recuse himself from this case if it were to come before the Supreme Court, since he had already sat as a judge on the case.

Senator Feingold asked that an article from *Slate* magazine by law professors Stephen Gillers, David Luban, and Steven Lubet concerning the legal requirements of Roberts to recuse him from the *Hamdan v. Rumsfeld* case as a result of being interviewed for a Supreme Court justice position be submitted into the record. The article by the three professors argued that:

...the interviews violated federal law on the disqualification of judges. Federal law—so critical that
it requires judges to step aside if their "impartiality
might reasonably be questioned," even if the judge is
completely impartial as a matter of fact. As Justice
John Paul Stevens wrote in a 1988 Supreme Court
opinion, "the very purpose of [this law] is to promote confidence in the judiciary by avoiding even
the appearance of impropriety whenever possible."
The requirement of an appearance of impartiality
has been cited in situations like the one here, leading
to the disqualification of a judge or the reversal of a
verdict.

The authors went on to cite cases where the conflict had been
similar to that of *Hamdan v. Rumsfeld*, but not as serious as that
case (either in the case itself or in the nature of the conflict),
where the verdict was reversed or the judge was disqualified.
There was very little news coverage of this blemish in Judge
Roberts's record. Senator Feingold asked that the professors'
article be put in the congressional record. Submitting the
article into the congressional record—but without detailed
questioning about its content, without the help of other senators to bring attention to these ethical issues, and without the
help of the corporate media to bring attention to the ethical issues, was not enough to bring the case to the public's
attention. The present process allows the Senate confirmation proceeding to take place without accountability to the
people.

Senator Feingold further questioned Roberts about his potential recusal:

> FEINGOLD: But when was the issue of whether you should recuse yourselves from this case—when did that first come to your attention?
> ROBERTS: I saw—was made aware of an article. I think it was an article. I don't remember when that took place. Whenever the article was published.
> FEINGOLD: You don't recall when this matter first came up? One would think it would be something you'd remember when somebody suggested you should have recused yourself.
> ROBERTS: I don't remember the date of the...
> FEINGOLD: How about the approximate time?
> ROBERTS: I think it was sometime in July.

The main issue of the *Hamdan* case before Judge Roberts was the legitimacy and fairness of the legal process. This issue did not get adequate coverage by the corporate media.

Chief Justice Rehnquist died on September 3, 2005, while Roberts's confirmation was still pending before the Senate. On September 5, President Bush withdrew Roberts's nomination as O'Connor's successor and instead announced Roberts's new nomination to the position of Chief Justice.

The following are representative of the corporate media's comments on Roberts:

Before his nomination, we suggested several criteria that Mr. Bush should adopt to garner broad bipartisan support: professional qualifications of the highest caliber, a modest conception of the judicial function, a strong belief in the stability of precedent, adherence to judicial philosophy, and an appreciation that fidelity to the text of the Constitution need not mean cramped interpretations of language that was written for a changing society. Judge Roberts possesses the personal qualities we hoped for and testified impressively as to his belief in the judicial values.
—The *Washington Post*, September 18, 2005

He made it clear at his hearings and in rulings from the federal bench that the court exists not to act—not even to react—but chiefly to interpret passively.
—The *New York Times*, October 21, 2005

Roberts was confirmed as Chief Justice by a full Senate vote of 78 to 22 on September 29, 2005. The above quotations are representative of most of the vetting process, the corporate written and TV media, and most of the senators' statements. Chief Justice Rehnquist wrote in his *2004 Year-end Report on the Federal Judiciary*:

Our Constitution has struck a balance between judicial independence and accountability, giving individual judges secure tenure, but making the federal judiciary subject ultimately to the popular will, because judges are appointed and confirmed by elected officials.

Today the balance that our Constitution struck "between judicial independence and accountability" has been carefully and thoughtfully deconstructed so that the federal judiciary is not ultimately subject to the popular will. The current state of the vetting process fails to provide the public with the information required for accountability. This is representative of government decision making in this time of the plutocracy's control of the electoral process.

The strategy for getting a corporate protector on the Supreme Court and keeping him/her there is to nominate a young lawyer-young because then the justice will be on the court for a long time-or an appeals court judge (preferably one who has not been a judge for very long) with a thin paper trail, and to keep any information from the public that would reveal to the Senate a preference on the part of the nominee to rule to protect the plutocracy's interests. Such a strategy is accomplished with the cooperation of the corporate media and senators. President Bush expressed a desire to clone Justices Scalia and Thomas; he did so with his nominations of Roberts and Alito.

As described above, Senator Feingold forcefully questioned Judge Roberts. Feingold had served eighteen years as the United States Senator from Wisconsin. Senator Feingold was a preeminent champion of reform who coauthored the aforementioned Bipartisan Campaign Reform Act of 2002 and had been one of the most outspoken critics of the war in Iraq and the *Citizens United* decision. One could be certain that he would be targeted in his next reelection.

Senator Feingold was only one of two incumbent senators who failed to be reelected in 2010. The other senator was Arlen Specter, who had switched from the Republican Party to the Democratic Party and was subsequently targeted by his former party. Senator Specter was not a reliable corporate protector—he was a Republican senator who had voted against Bork during his Supreme Court confirmation.

This effective targeting of senators who fail in their role to protect corporate interests and fail to work to enhance the plutocracy's control of the electoral process has a double benefit for the corporate protectors—the plutocracy silences opponents in the Senate and sends a clear message about the consequences of speaking out to others who might want to speak out for an open government and accountability to the people.

The proposed PMB would provide the necessary complementary discussions to the Senate confirmation hearings as part of the confirmation process, discussions which are conducted by persons free of the political pressures of loyalty to party, incumbency, and format dictated by the political party bosses. It is essential that there be access to and discussion of previous performance in office and about the nominee's judicial philosophy: how he or she views the role of the court in shaping the electoral process, in shaping the political conversation, and in limiting the role of Congress as the people's representatives in reaching the compromises that need to be made between the corporate interests and the people's interests. The Public Media Board will make it possible for the people to gain the information they need to hold elected officials accountable. These steps are part of the broader process of taking control of the electoral process and enabling meaningful voting that is based on information.

Section 14: Repealing *Citizens United*

14(a). We the people, who ordain and establish this Constitution, intend the rights protected by this Constitution to be the rights of natural persons.

14(b). The words *people, person,* or *citizen* as used in this Constitution do not include corporations, limited liability companies, or any other corporate entities established by the laws of any state, the federal government of the United States, or any foreign state. Such corporate entities are subject to such regulation as the people (through their elected state and federal representatives) deem reasonable and that are otherwise consistent with the powers of Congress and the states under this Constitution.

14(c). Nothing contained herein shall be construed to limit the people's rights of freedom of speech, freedom of the press, free exercise of religion, freedom of association, or any other such rights of the people, as these rights are inalienable. Congress shall have the power to make all laws necessary and appropriate to carry into effect all the foregoing sections of this Voters' Rights Amendment.

On January 21, 2015 Rep. McGovern of Massachusetts introduced the above joint resolution, which was referred to committee.

Reasons for Section 14

In 2002, Congress passed the Bipartisan Campaign Reform Act (often called the McCain-Feingold Act or "BCRA"). The act was ruled to be consistent with the Constitution by the Supreme Court in *McConnell v. FEC* (2003). The majority opinion stated that:

> More than a century ago the "sober-minded Elihu Root" advocated legislation that would prohibit political contributions by corporations in order to prevent "the great aggregations of wealth, from using their corporate funds, directly or indirectly" to elect legislators who would "vote for their protection and the advancement of their interests as against those of the public." In Root's opinion, such legislation would "strike at a constantly growing evil which has done more to shake the confidence of the plain people of small means of this country in our political institutions than any other practice which has ever obtained since the foundation of our Government." The Congress of the United States has repeatedly enacted legislation endorsing Root's judgment. [Internal citations omitted].

In his dissent, Justice Scalia commented:

> The last proposition that might explain at least some of today's casual abridgment of free-speech rights is this: that the particular form of association known as a corporation does not enjoy full First Amendment protection. Of course the text of the First Amendment does

not limit its application in this fashion, even though "[b]y the end of the eighteenth century the corporation was a familiar figure in American economic life." Nor is there any basis in reason why First Amendment rights should not attach to corporate associations.

Starting in the late 1800s and continuing to the present, tens of thousands of pages have been recorded of legislative investigations and testimony about the corrupting influence of corporate money in the elections of federal officials, and testimony of its corrupting influence on federal officials' performance in office. In addition, thousands of pages of laws regulating corporate spending have been written to limit corporate control of governmental functioning, and several court cases have found these laws to be constitutional. Despite this history, Justice Scalia, (as noted above) maintains that there is "no basis in reason why First Amendment rights should not attach to corporate association," thus preventing Congress from passing laws that would regulate the "corporate speech" that influences the electoral process. The First Amendment states, in part, that:

Congress shall make no law respecting an establishment of religion, or prohibiting the free exercise thereof; or abridging the freedom of speech, or of the press; or the right of the people peaceably to assemble, and to petition the Government for a redress of grievances.

One guiding judicial principle for five justices is the protection and enhancement of their corporate brethren's "free exercise of their religion": the religion whose uniting tenet is to protect their God-given right, their Constitutional right, to make money, and to make more money with governmental help, with minimal taxation, minimal regulatory interference, and with financial support. The establishment of the corporate religion, and the government enhancement of that religion, has allowed the corporate brethren to achieve immortality by magically morphing—fusing the body parts of other corporate bodies into monsters that are too big to die, and too big to fail—corporations that are big enough to secure profits by favorable governmental regulations, and big enough to stay alive by huge injections of tax dollars if corporate greed gets them into financial difficulties.

Citizens United v. FCC, McCutcheon v. FEC, and other decisions have removed virtually any semblance of campaign finance reform. These decisions make it illegal for Congress to pass laws that would protect the electoral process from the corruption of corporations buying political influence.

The people's First Amendment right-"The right of the people peaceably to assemble, and to petition the Government for a redress of grievances"—is denied by corporate personhood's money rights; the money rights that have become the dominant force in the democratic process. The role of money in electing corporate protectors is often downplayed in the media. The quote below is from an op-ed piece by David Brooks in the *New York Times*, from October 9, 2014:

> The final and most important effect of *Citizens United* is that it will reduce the influence of money on electoral outcomes. Yes, that's right. Reduce... money is not that important in high-attention federal races... every plausible Senate candidate and almost every plausible House candidate has more than enough money to get his or her message [across].

There is truth to this statement when one looks at the influence of money in the electoral process in terms of the outcome of the primary process which almost invariably results in a general election between a well-funded Republican and well-funded Democrat, both beholden to corporate money.

The corrupting influence on the electoral process goes well beyond the effects of the *Citizens United* decision. The repeal of *Citizens United* and a constitutional amendment that would declare that corporations are not persons would be an essential step in the reform of the electoral process, but it is not a sufficient step in the effort to make the electoral process healthy and elected officials accountable to the voters for their governmental decisions.

Summary Comments on the VRA

Taking control of the electoral process from the plutocracy is similar to the Civil Rights movement in the 1950s; the goal in both cases was seeking the rights of full citizenship for people whose rights have been denied. In the successful Civil Rights movement during the 1950s and 60s, it was essential to move from addressing a few aspects of discrimination to insisting on delegitimizing the entire system of segregation including but not limited to making it difficult or impossible for black citizens to vote. To be successful in taking control of the electoral process from the plutocracy, it will necessary to remove all of the plutocracy's methods of control of the electoral process and not just focus on a few aspects of that control.

In 1948, in Clarendon County, South Carolina, Thurgood Marshall, a young NAACP lawyer at the time, filed a petition in the US District Court seeking a ruling that black children should be provided with school bus transportation—black children had to walk to school, sometimes many miles, while white children rode buses. The white superintendent of the schools said that black citizens did not pay enough taxes to support a bus, and that asking white taxpayers to do this would be unfair. This was a case where money talks, the black children walk, and their parents do not get to vote. The case was dismissed on technical grounds.

With the encouragement and help of the state and national NAACP, Marshall sought a case that would go beyond mere transportation and would ask for equal educational opportunities in Clarendon County. Federal District Court Judge Waties Waring intimated that he wanted a case that would do more than ask for equal facilities: he wanted a case that would challenge the entire notion of "separate but equal," the existing law under the 1896 *Plessy v. Ferguson* Supreme Court decision that upheld state laws that *require* racial segregation in public facilities.

Several appeals court cases came before the Supreme Court in 1952; the court consolidated the cases under the name of *Brown v. Board of Education of Topeka*. Marshall personally argued the case before the court. The real issue was that as long as separation exists, schools will be unequal. Marshall argued that separate school systems for blacks and whites were inherently unequal, and thus violated the Equal Protection Clause of the Fourteenth Amendment to the US Constitution. Relying on studies that a sociologist had conducted, Marshall maintained that segregated school systems had a tendency to make black children feel inferior to white children. On May 14, 1954, Chief Justice Warren delivered the opinion of the court, stating:

We conclude that in the field of public education the doctrine of "separate but equal" has no place. Separate educational facilities are inherently unequal...

We conclude that our two-political-party electoral process, bought, paid for by the plutocracy is inherently unequal. If you do not want to run for office as a Democrat or a Republican, if you do not feel comfortable supporting either the Democratic or Republican candidate, and if the issues you are most concerned about are not being addressed, then you have little opportunity to meaningfully join others and to "peaceably...assemble, to meaningfully petition the Government for a redress of grievances."

As long as the plutocracy controls the electoral process, the opportunities to run for political office, petition the government for the redress of grievances, and vote meaningfully will be inherently unequal. As long as separation exists on the political playing field between third-party candidates and candidates of the two main political parties, the electoral process will be inherently unequal.

During the 1950s, 60s, and 70s, the Supreme Court helped the country address the challenges of that period. Congress worked to consider and pass laws that were designed to address the challenges of ensuring full citizenship and to expand suffrage. For the last two decades, however, the Supreme Court has become part of the problem by weakening and hampering the democratic processes by restricting Congress's ability to address the various challenges the nation faces, and by declaring effective protections of the right to vote to be unconstitutional. Congress and the executive branch of government have cooperated in this by allowing the mainstream media to consolidate (and be controlled by) a small group of corporate executives, by holding sham Supreme Court confirmation hearings, and by cooperating with the corporate agenda by actively pursuing gridlock: gridlock that allows lawmakers to avoid discussing any laws that would balance the corporate interests with the people's interests. Combining gridlock with the corrupted electoral process allows elected officials to be corporate-interest protectors and avoid accountability to the voters.

In order to free the electoral process of control by the plutocracy, it will be essential to consider all of the mechanisms of the plutocracy's control of the electoral process. *Citizens United v. FCC* would not have happened if the plutocracy had not already had substantial control of the electoral process, the nomination and approval of Supreme Court justices, and government decision making before that decision. Broadening the proposed amendment to repeal the *Citizen United* decision to include corrective measures that would address all of the methods of the plutocracy's control will work to clarify the full picture of the plutocracy's control, will change and strengthen the arguments for the amendment, will broaden the base of support for the amendment, and will help to produce the necessary passion to successfully reform our political process.

After the deliberations of the Constitutional Convention in 1787, a Mrs. Powel of Philadelphia asked Benjamin

Franklin, "Well, Doctor, what have we got, a republic or a monarchy?" Franklin responded, "A republic, if you can keep it."

To restore and protect our republic, we need to send a message to our legislators (and candidates for election), "You must vote for the proposed Voters' Rights Amendment, or you will not be reelected!"

About the Authors

John Kellett, PhD, mathematics, University of Florida (1968), and professor emeritus at Gettysburg College, is the principal author of this book. He served as a naval officer (1959–1963) at Sandia Base, New Mexico. He instructed officers from all military branches who had been assigned to nuclear weapons duty on nuclear weapons design, safety, policy, and possible use. After receiving his PhD, he joined the mathematics department at Gettysburg College, where he taught from 1968 to 1999. In addition to teaching mathematics, he taught courses on nuclear weaponry; the political, official, and media discussions of the rationale for particular weapons; the possible use of nuclear weapons; and the threat of using nuclear weapons. In their article in *Polity*, he and his colleague Kenneth Mott, professor of political science at Gettysburg College, were among the first authors to suggest approval voting as an electoral reform in the 1970s.

Christine Hunter Kellett, JD, Dickinson School of Law (1975), and professor emerita, Dickinson School of Law at Pennsylvania

State University, collaborated with her husband on this book. She taught constitutional law at Dickinson from 1976 to 2004, as well as courses on government law and the United States Supreme Court.

Made in the USA
Middletown, DE
09 April 2016